Worship God

Worship God

WATCHMAN NEE

Christian Fellowship Publishers, Inc.
New York

ISBN 0-935008-73-X

Available from the publishers at:

11515 Allecingie Parkway
Richmond, Virginia 23235

PRINTED IN U.S.A.

EDITOR'S PREFACE

"Thou shalt worship the Lord thy God, and him only shalt thou serve" (Matt. 4.10). This is the principal duty of man. God alone is worthy to be worshipped. But this prerogative of God is fiercely contested in the universe. Satan tries to rob God of His worship, and man is tempted to worship anything other than God himself. The Lord Jesus came into this world to restore worship to God. He declared: "the hour cometh, and now is, when the true worshippers shall worship the Father in spirit and truth: for such doth the Father seek to be his worshippers" (John 4.23). As the redeemed children of God, we now have the privilege of being true worshippers. It is therefore imperative for us to know what worship is and how we should worship. This missing jewel must be recovered in the Church.

In Part One of this volume, Watchman Nee lays down the axiom that worship belongs to God. He explains how worship comes only by revelation and how it must be done in spirit and in truth. He further illustrates the battle of the ages over worship and how eventually God will receive the worship of men. To worship God is to worship His ways. Therefore, let us worship Him under whatever circumstances.

Then in parts Two and Three, the author deals with various subjects such as spiritual conflict, spiritual reality, the offence of the Lord, and so forth.

May God use this book to prepare for himself a people who are true worshippers.

CONTENTS

PART ONE

FROM THE MINISTRY OF 1939–40*

*Being a reproduction of the notes—taken down in English by a dear Christian sister now with the Lord—of the author's messages on Worship delivered in Chinese during this period, with no more than some necessary tidying up added.—*Editor*

1 | Worship Belongs to God

Thou shalt have no other gods before me. Thou shalt not make unto thee a graven image, nor any likeness of any thing that is in heaven above, or that is in the earth beneath, or that is in the water under the earth: thou shalt not bow down thyself unto them, nor serve them; for I Jehovah thy God am a jealous God, visiting the iniquity of the fathers upon the children, upon the third and upon the fourth generation of them that hate me, and showing lovingkindness unto thousands of them that love me and keep my commandments. Thou shalt not take the name of Jehovah thy God in vain; for Jehovah will not hold him guiltless that taketh his name in vain. Remember the sabbath day, to keep it holy. (Ex. 20.3–8)

Thou shalt worship no other god: for Jehovah, whose name is Jealous, is a jealous God. (Ex. 34.14)

Take ye therefore good heed unto yourselves; for ye saw no manner of form on the day that Jehovah spoke unto you in Horeb out of the midst of the fire; lest ye corrupt yourselves, and make you a graven image in the

Worship God

form of any figure, the likeness of male or female, the likeness of any beast that is on the earth, the likeness of any winged bird that flieth in the heavens, the likeness of any thing that creepeth on the ground, the likeness of any fish that is in the water under the earth; and lest thou lift up thine eyes unto heaven, and when thou seest the sun and the moon and the stars, even all the host of them, thou be drawn away and worship them, and serve them, which Jehovah thy God hath allotted unto all the peoples under the whole heaven. (Deut. 4.15–19)

But if thy heart turn away, and thou wilt not hear, but shalt be drawn away, and worship other gods, and serve them; I denounce unto you this day, that ye shall surely perish; ye shall not prolong your days in the land, whither thou passest over the Jordan to go in to possess it. I call heaven and earth to witness against you this day, that I have set before thee life and death, the blessing and the curse: therefore choose life, that thou mayest live, thou and thy seed. (Deut. 30.17–19)

But if ye shall turn away from following me, ye or your children, and not keep my commandments and my statutes which I have set before you, but shall go and serve other gods, and worship them; then will I cut off Israel out of the land which I have given them; and this house, which I have hallowed for my name, will I cast out of my sight; and Israel shall be a proverb and a byword among all peoples. . . . and they shall answer, Because they forsook Jehovah their God, who brought forth their fathers out of the land of Egypt, and laid hold on other gods, and worshipped them, and served them: therefore hath Jehovah brought all this evil upon them. (1 Kings 9.6–7,9)

And all the assembly worshipped, and the singers sang,

and the trumpeters sounded; all this continued until the burnt-offering was finished. And when they had made an end of offering, the king and all that were present with him bowed themselves and worshipped. Moreover Hezekiah the king and the princes commanded the Levites to sing praises unto Jehovah with the words of David, and of Asaph the seer. And they sang praises with gladness, and they bowed their heads and worshipped. (2 Chron. 29.28–30)

And they stood up in their place, and read in the book of the law of Jehovah their God a fourth part of the day; and another fourth part they confessed, and worshipped Jehovah their God. ... Thou art Jehovah, even thou alone; thou hast made heaven, the heaven of heavens, with all their host, the earth and all things that are thereon, the seas and all that is in them, and thou preserveth them all; and the host of heaven worshippeth thee. (Neh. 9.3,6)

Where is he that is born King of the Jews? for we saw his star in the east, and are come to worship him. ... And they came into the house and saw the young child with Mary his mother; and they fell down and worshipped him; and opening their treasures they offered unto him gifts, gold and frankincense and myrrh. (Matt. 2.2,11)

And he [the devil] said unto him, All these things will I give thee, if thou wilt fall down and worship me. Then saith Jesus unto him, Get thee hence, Satan: for it is written, Thou shalt worship the Lord thy God, and him only shalt thou serve. (Matt. 4.9–10)

The four and twenty elders shall fall down before him that sitteth on the throne, and shall worship him that liveth for ever and ever, and shall cast their crowns before the throne, saying, Worthy art thou, our Lord and our God, to receive the glory and the honor and the power: for thou didst create all things, and because of thy will they were, and were created. (Rev. 4.10–11)

And the four living creatures said, Amen. And the elders fell down and worshipped. (Rev. 5.14)

And I John am he that heard and saw these things. And when I heard and saw, I fell down to worship before the feet of the angel that showed me these things. And he saith unto me, See thou do it not: I am a fellow-servant with thee and with thy brethren the prophets, and with them that keep the words of this book: worship God. (Rev. 22.8–9)

The temptation of Jesus in the wilderness reveals the importance of worship, the importance of worshipping the Creator. Many place more importance on Savior than on Creator. It is true that we must first recognize the Savior in order to know the Lord as God. Yet it is not enough to know only His redeeming work, since His redeeming work is to lead men to know Him as Creator. The Blood is first in *order*, but it is not first in *importance*. God's purpose is not just that we should know the Savior. The Righteous died for the unrighteous to lead us to God (see 1 Peter 3.18).

What are God's demands in His word? There are the Ten Commandments. The first four are concerned with God himself. About 2500 years separate the Creation of Man and Sinai. With respect to this long interval, we basically have only the books of Job and Genesis that recount the story. Job is a private history, whereas Genesis provides a general history. Yet neither of them tells us God's purpose; in neither of them had God revealed why He had made man. Also, we do not really know from these accounts why the Devil came and tempted man. Genesis does not tell us what God was after when He made man. And Genesis 3 does not tell us what the Devil ultimately desired to accomplish by his tempting man.

However, once God had delivered His people from Egypt and had given them the Ten Commandments, we thereafter know why God indeed made man and what He wanted. The Ten Commandments are precious, for they show us God's heart. It is not surprising that God wrote them twice. For the first time in about 2500 years He at last told man at Sinai what He had been after in creating him. Furthermore, God saw to it that the book of Deuteronomy would repeat the record of His commands.

"Thou shalt have no other gods before me [or, besides me]" (Ex. 20.3). Deuteronomy adds to this first commandment these words: "Thou shalt fear [worship] Jehovah thy God, and him [only] shalt thou serve" (6.13; cf. this with Matt. 4.10). Hence, from this, man learns for the first time that God desires worship.

What is the meaning of worship? In Hebrew, the word means to kneel and worship. In Greek, it means to go forward and kiss His hand. In other words, to give everything to Him.

Many do not know the secret of worshipping God. The Lord, He is *God*. Jesus is *God*. This is very precious. God wants man to declare that He *is* God. The Lord taught the disciples to pray. The Lord's Prayer is connected with the Ten Commandments. In that prayer

He told the disciples what God wanted: "Hallowed be thy name" (Matt. 6.9b). What does God hope for first? What do Jesus' words here mean? "Hallowedness" or holiness means to be set apart for God. The name of God is hallowed, is holy. It belongs to God, and God's name can be used by God alone. This is the meaning of "hallowed be thy name." Now, though, His name is being used by others. Now it has become general and common. But one day it will be specific and holy. Only Jehovah will be called God. Nothing else will be called by that Name. God's demand of men is that they know Him as *God*.

After the resurrection the Lord spoke to Mary (and by extension, of course, to all His disciples): "... my Father and your Father, and my God and your God" (John 20.17b). "Father" speaks of one's individual relationship, while "God" speaks of a universal relationship.

What is worship? It is confessing Him as *God*. Among the Old Testament books, Deuteronomy especially stresses this matter of worshipping God. Worship *God*; you cannot worship anything else. If you worship anything else you will die. If anyone worships idols he will be stoned to death. God does not permit the worship of ought else but himself.

What is the work of the Devil? From the account in Genesis of the garden of Eden, we really cannot discern what the work of the Devil is. But Isaiah 14.12–14 at last reveals to us that the Devil wants to be like God. And later, the Gospel of Matthew chapter 4 shows us even further what his object has always been. Matthew 4 records how the Devil tempted the Lord Jesus three times. The first two temptations held no special advantage for him. But in the third one the Enemy finally came out with, "Worship me." In response, though, the Lord Jesus took the word from Deuteronomy, saying, "Thou shalt worship the Lord thy God." All this indicates that the Devil has wanted worship. God wants worship, and the Devil also wants worship. All worship of idols is worship of Satan. Why does Satan fear the salvation of men? Because they will worship God. Hence, he hates for men to be saved.

When we come to the book of Revelation, we find described there special events which must come to pass. A particular line of worship runs through Revelation. From chapters 4 and 5 to chapter 19, we learn that the twenty-four elders and the four living creatures worship in heaven. But in chapter 13 we see worship of the image of the beast on earth. Satan wants to obtain what God is getting above, for Satan's purpose is not only to make men sin but also to make them worship him. To worship him is sin, and his satanic kingdom is stengthened by worship. This will be Satan's happiest day. The Antichrist will call himself God (see 2 Thess. 2.4). This is what Satan has wanted throughout these six thousand years. Worship of the beast is worship of Satan.

In Revelation chapter 13 we find that the beast wants worship. In chapter 14 we see that the eternal gospel is preached: "Fear God, and give him glory; for the hour of his judgment is come: and worship him that made the heaven and the earth and sea and fountains of waters" (v.7). Worship God—this is the eternal gospel. In chapters 21 and 22 we have the new heaven and the new earth. Again we are commanded to worship God (22.9).

Since God's purpose is worship and Satan's purpose is also worship, what is the duty of us Christians? It is not enough just to know salvation. What is it that will satisfy God? Who will satisfy Him? Not those who are only able to pray or to preach, but those who are able to worship Him. We must put worship into everything we do. This, in fact, is the characteristic of the Dohnavur Fellowship in India.* There is always this note of worship at Dohnavur.

Satan fears the worship of God. Let us put worship first. Do you have difficulties? First worship God. Worship by the few today is giving God what He will one day have from all. The Church is the first fruits of God's creatures (see James 1.18). What the world will one day give God, we first give Him. We do not wait till in the new heaven and new earth to worship. In this old heaven and old earth we worship today. At this time we want to give special worship to the Lord, for Satan is more and more getting worship for himself. If we are defeated in worship we shall be defeated in other things.

---

*The Dohnavur Fellowship is a work that was raised up by God at the beginning of this present century in the small village of Dohnavur near the southern tip of India through the instrumentality of Amy Carmichael. It is a rescue work for Indian boys and girls in moral danger. For its history, read *Amy Carmichael of Dohnavur* by Bishop Frank Houghton and *Gold Cord* by Amy Carmichael, both originally published by S.P.C.K. Publishers, London, but now published and available from Christian Literature Crusade, Ft. Washington, PA (USA), Canada, Great Britain and elsewhere.—*Editor*

2 | Worship Comes through Revelation

All the earth shall worship thee, and shall sing unto thee; they shall sing to thy name. (Ps. 66.4)

All nations whom thou hast made shall come and worship before thee, O Lord; and they shall glorify thy name. For thou art great, and doest wondrous things: thou art God alone. (Ps. 86.9–10)

It shall come to pass, that from one new moon to another, and from one sabbath to another, shall all flesh come to worship before me, saith Jehovah. (Is. 66.23)

It shall come to pass, that every one that is left of all the nations that came against Jerusalem shall go up from year to year to worship the King, Jehovah of hosts, and to keep the feast of tabernacles. And it shall be, that whoso of all the families of the earth goeth not up unto Jerusalem to worship the King, Jehovah of hosts, upon them there shall be no rain. (Zech. 14.16–17)

It shall come to pass in that day, that a great trumpet shall be blown; and they shall come that were ready to perish in the land of Assyria, and they that were outcasts in the land of Egypt; and they shall worship Jehovah in the holy mountain at Jerusalem. (Is. 27.13)

Hath not the same Hezekiah taken away his high places and his altars, and commanded Judah and Jerusalem, saying, Ye shall worship before one altar, and upon it shall ye burn incense? (2 Chron. 32.12)

Ascribe unto Jehovah the glory due unto his name; worship Jehovah in holy array. (Ps. 29.2)

But as for me, in the abundance of thy lovingkindness will I come into thy house: in thy fear will I worship toward thy holy temple. (Ps. 5.7)

The object of Creation is that God might receive worship. But the object of the Devil's work is also to receive worship. As we saw earlier, the Ten Commandments reveal God's heart. Without them we do not know God's heart or His demands. What actually are idols? That outside of God there is something else to worship.

Through idolatry Israel lost her position as a nation of priests. Only the Levites from among the Israelites could now have that position of priests. The most serious punishment is not to go to hell, but to lose the *ministry* of the priest. For when God loses His portion, His people lose their portion as well—their blessings. In Canaan there soon came into existence high places, altars, and other gods. The result was the dispersion of Israel. Later, the greatest revival in the history of Judah came under King Hezekiah. What kind of revival was it? Worship was recovered. The next revival came under Nehemiah after the return of the Jewish remnant. It was also a revival of worship.

Then Jesus came onto the scene. In Matthew 2 we learn that the wise men came to worship. Only those who had *eyes* could see that that small child was God. One of the greatest revelations of the New Testament occurred during the temptation of Jesus in the wilderness, for a right understanding of this event can open our eyes to see what Satan's object has always been: man's worship of him. In our hearts we have something which God wants and which Satan also wants. What heaven wants, hell too wants. Heaven and hell fight for it—worship. Two thrones are at war. What are they fighting over? Worship.

Matthew especially shows us Jesus as King. So it especially speaks of those who worshipped Him. The Lord Jesus received what God should always receive from His people God wants to get a people for himself who *know* Him. God desires to get a *people* for himself, not just *children*. Of course, we must first know the Father in order to know God. Our spiritual beginning is obviously at the Blood, and then we can know God.

To know Him as Father is a personal relationship, but to know Him as God is knowing His official and exalted standing in the universe. Many know Him as Father, but they do not know Him as God. What is worship? It is simply this: that I recognize that He is God and that I am but a man. When I see Him as Father, I am *saved*. When I see Him as God, *I* am finished and done with. For when we see Him as God, we can only fall down humbly and worship. The whole matter rests upon our seeing. Worship does not arise from the Blood—as precious as the Latter is; worship comes only from seeing. It does not come because we see doctrine.

It is revelation. Praise and worship is something objective, thanksgiving is something subjective. *Know the
Father* and the heart will be filled with joy. *Know
God* and the heart will be filled with glory. Glory cannot be explained, but those who see God know what
glory is.

Let me illustrate this with an experience from the
life of Mrs. Jessie Penn-Lewis. From her biography we
learn that she was seeking for the enduement of power
from on high. "Then two or three searching questions
were put to me by the Spirit of God. The first was: 'If
I answer your cry, are you willing to be unpopular?'
Unpopular! Be rejected? Well yes, I am willing. I have
never faced it before, but I am willing. Why did I desire
the fullness of the Spirit? Was it for success in service,
and that I should be considered a much-used worker?
Would I desire the same fullness of the Spirit if it meant
apparent failure, and becoming the off-scouring of all
things in the eyes of others? This had not occurred to
me before, and I quickly agreed to any conditions the
Lord should please to set before me.

"Again came the question:—Would I be willing to
have no great experience, but agree to live and walk entirely by faith in the Word of God? ... Yes! These were
the questions put to me by God, and then the matter
dropped.

"Then came the climax, when one morning I awoke,
and lo, I beheld before me a hand holding up in terrible light a handful of filthy rags, whilst a gentle voice
said: 'This is the outcome of all our past service for
God.' 'But Lord, I have been surrendered and consecrated to thee all these years: It was consecrated work!'

'Yes, my child, but all your service has been *consecrated self*: the outcome of your own energy: your own plans for winning souls: your own devotion. All for Me, I grant you, but *yourself*, all the same.'

"The unveiling was truly a horror to me, and brought me in deep abasement to the Blood of Christ for cleansing. Then came the still, small voice once more, and this time it was the one little word— 'Crucified'!

"Crucified—what did it mean? I had not asked to be crucified, but to be filled. But now Romans 6.6-11 became a power to me, and I knew the meaning of 'our old man was crucified with Him ...' and what Paul meant in his words, 'crucified with Christ' (Gal. 2.20).

"As a little child, I rested on the word thus given, and then it 'pleased the Lord to reveal His Son in me that I might preach Him'—I knew the Risen Lord."

This revelation of the Risen Lord came to Mrs. Penn-Lewis suddenly and unexpectedly, explained her biographer; it was not in an hour of "waiting" upon God, nor in a meeting with others seeking the same blessing; but, at the breakfast table in her own home one morning in March, the glory of the Lord was revealed in her spirit—even as it was to Paul on his way to Damascus—and with such blinding power that she fled to her own room to fall upon her knees in worship and speechless adoration. *

In 2 Corinthians 5.11 we have these precious words

---

*See Mary N. Garrard, *Jessie Penn-Lewis—A Memoir* (Westbourne, England: Overcomer Book Room, Second Edition, 1947), pp. 24–26. The first edition was published in 1930.—*Editor* of Paul: "Knowing therefore the fear [or, terror] of the Lord." God is lovable, but He is also to be feared. The proud do not know God. Those who condemn others have not seen Him. True humility comes from seeing God. Having known God, that humility cannot be moved. It needs new revelation and deep knowledge of God; otherwise, many things are merely doctrine.

"Ascribe unto Jehovah the glory due unto his name; worship Jehovah in holy array" (Ps. 29.2). "But as for me, in the abundance of thy lovingkindness will I come into thy house: in thy fear will I worship toward thy holy temple" (Ps. 5.7). These two verses show us that there are two things needful in worship—holiness and fear. In holy splendor, worship God. No one who has seen God can allow sin or any unrighteousness in his life. When we appear before people, the first thing we think of is our dress. It is the same in our appearing before God. We must worship Him in the beauty of holiness. Those who live under the glory of God always say, "I am a sinner."

Then there is the matter of the fear of God. One who sees God fears Him, for my God "is a consuming fire" (Heb. 12.29). So, fear Him. Everything that can be burned, He *will* burn. It is dangerous for those who do not know the work of the cross to meet God. But with all who have had drastic dealing by the cross, God cannot consume them, just as fire could not consume Daniel's three God-devoted companions in the fiery furnace (see Daniel 3). If one has seen God, the fear of God is a natural thing.

What should we do, since God wants worship and Satan also wants worship? Let us worship *God*. The whole life of God's people should be a life of worship. Begin each day of life with worship.

Remember worship in all matters of life. The more we worship, the more reason we will have to worship Him. The more you know what eternity is, the more you will know what worship is. Never begin anything without first worshipping God. First give Him His portion. If the church gives God His portion of worship in everything, it will eventually result in God's worship being established in the whole earth.

In the new heaven and the new earth all flesh shall worship God. Now, though, He does not receive worship of all, but only of those who *will* worship Him. Yes, we are not to look lightly upon work, prayer, and so forth; even so, let us esteem worship even more highly. Our note throughout our lives should be one of worship continually.

3 | Worship in Spirit

God created man in his own image, in the image of God created he him; male and female created he them. (Gen. 1.27)

Jehovah God formed man of the dust of the ground, and breathed into his nostrils the breath of life; and man became a living soul. (Gen. 2.7)

Blessed are the poor in spirit; for theirs is the kingdom of heaven. (Matt. 5.3)

He that doth not take his cross and follow after me, is not worthy of me. He that findeth his [soul] life shall lose it; and he that loseth his [soul] life for my sake shall find it. (Matt. 10.38–39)

The woman saith unto him, Sir, I perceive that thou art a prophet. Our fathers worshipped in this mountain; and ye say, that in Jerusalem is the place where men ought to worship. Jesus saith unto her, Woman, believe me, the hour cometh, when neither in this mountain, nor in Jerusalem, shall ye worship the Father. Ye worship that which ye know not: we worship that which we know; for salvation is from the Jews. But the hour cometh, and now is, when the true worshippers shall worship the Father in spirit and truth: for such doth the Father seek to be his worshippers. God is a Spirit: and they that worship him must worship in spirit and truth. (John 4.19–24)

Now the natural man receiveth not the things of the Spirit of God: for they are foolishness unto him; and he cannot know them, because they are spiritually judged. (1 Cor. 2.14)

Behold your calling, brethren, that not many wise after the flesh, not many mighty, not many noble, are called: but God chose the foolish things of the world, that he might put to shame them that are wise; and God chose the weak things of the world, that he might put to shame the things that are strong; and the base things of the world, and the things that are despised, did God choose, yea and the things that are not, that he might bring to nought the things that are. (1 Cor. 1.26–28)

He that is joined unto the Lord is one spirit. (1 Cor. 6.17)

If we want to understand worship we must understand John 4. It is necessary to know that New Testament passage in order to worship. A special question is raised: what is the relationship between worship and man's creation? Just to be a Christian is too small, because there is a much larger issue in view.

According to John 4.24, "God is a Spirit: and they that worship him must worship in spirit ..." The fact of the matter is that since God is Spirit we must use spirit to worship Him. Thus the creation of man is important. If God desires worship He must form man with a spirit. The creation of man is unlike all the rest of creation. Man's constitution has a part that is like God's constitution. If man has a question about spirit, then worship also entails a question.

In 1 Corinthians 6.17 Paul writes: "he that is joined unto the Lord is one spirit." If you pour water into water, all is water. You cannot mix water with oil. As we are joined to the Lord, we do not become one body, but one spirit. Only spirit can touch God who is Spirit. When God created man, He placed, among other elements, a spirit in man. It is *that* part of man that is especially like God. Man has an element in him that is particularly like an element of God: God is Spirit, and so, too, a little part of us is spirit. * It is like my standing on the seashore: I finish here, and yet the sea begins here too. That little part of us called spirit can touch God and touch eternity. The lower creatures have feeling, and they can decide; but they cannot worship because they have no spirit. For this reason, man is very precious. Although when compared to the rest of all

---

*That God created man with more than spirit is made clear from Gen. 2.7: "dust of the ground (body), "the breath of life" (spirit), and "became a living soul" (soul—i.e., mind, emotion, will, etc.) But it is the spirit in man, according to the author, that is most akin to God and is that which is able to touch Him intimately. For a thorough discussion of these various elements in the whole man, and the relationship among them, the reader can consult Watchman Nee, *The Spiritual Man*, 3 vols. (New York: Christian Fellowship Publishers, originally translated from the Chinese and published in 1968; but a Combined (3 vols-in-1) Edition, 1977 is now the only format of the book available from the Publishers).—*Editor*

God's creation he appears to be rather insignificant, he is nonetheless a special creation.

However, if man wants to use his spirit to worship God, he must live in the spirit. He must preserve fellowship with God and maintain communication with Him.

Take a closer look at the fall of man. To say it was only an outside action is wrong. For by man's fall there was caused to take place a change in human constitution. What was the consequence of taking the forbidden fruit? Man's will was marred, his feeling became mixed, and his thoughts and attitudes changed. He himself—apart from God—could understand the difference between good and evil. When Adam and Eve sinned they underwent a change in their very constitution as it had originally been made by God. Before the Fall man had a spirit which could touch God. After the Fall his spirit died. Sin influences the human constitution; and thus man, as it were, became a different being. He was constitutionally changed. By the Fall in the garden of Eden, man added decisive powers to his soul.

If Satan wants worship, he must have something within man to worship him. Man can worship Satan in the soul. If I want something to worship me, I must raise it to life. A desk cannot worship me; I must change it. Satan! What does this name mean? Satan did not keep his original position—for he said, "I will be like God." As we know, spirit can only live by Spirit. It must have the life of God by which to live and to be nourished. After Satan sinned, his own fellowship with God was cut off. His small "I" became sin. Here we must see the difference between spirit and soul. Soul can decide: soul can decide to be independent. And hence, man can be independent of God. Thus Satan received worship from man. This is the profound meaning of what happened in Eden.

After man had eaten the forbidden fruit in Eden he did not need to refer everything to God. Before that, everything had to be referred to Him. Now, though, it was not necessary to refer things back to God. He had no need to pray. Instead, man now declared, "I can decide." Man in his creation had never inherited the power to decide. From this time, however, his constitution had drastically changed: he became an independent being, no longer dependent upon God. Just as the spirit and dependence are united, so the soul and independence are united. The man as originally created by God was of no use to Satan. For man to be useful to him, Satan must have proud men, independent men. And if man comes to live by the soul, his attitude will become one of arrogance.

True worship is when man stands in his position and God is in His. I as a man have limits, but God is unlimited. Every means is being used today to enlarge men's souls. This generation of men is special. Satan wants men who can do everything. For this particular reason, we must learn how to live by our spirit and ask the Lord to deliver us from the overbearing power of the soul. Whereas the spiritual are humble, the soulish are proud.

What is salvation? Salvation deals not only with sins but also with my constitution. I am both outwardly wrong and inwardly wrong. "That which is born of the Spirit is spirit" (John 3.6). It is regeneration of constitution. When a man is saved he is changed. Man's original fall was a matter of constitution, so regeneration is also a matter of constitution. The part of me that is soul cannot understand God. Only spirit can understand Him. Therefore, I must learn to lose my soul life. Our daily work is to lose our soul life. The substitutionary work of our Lord on the cross does not deal with our soul. We are to lose our own soul life by bearing the cross daily (see Matt. 10.38–39). What does it mean to lose the soul life? We come to God and learn not to judge anything by ourselves.

"Behold your calling, brethren, that not many wise after the flesh, not many mighty, not many noble, are called: but God chose the foolish things of the world, that he might put to shame them that are wise; and God chose the weak things of the world, that he might put to shame the things that are strong; and the base things of the world, and the things that are despised, did God choose, yea and the things that are not, that he might bring to nought the things that are" (1 Cor. 1.26–28). Why does God choose the foolish, the weak and the base? Because their souls are not enlarged. If we live after the spirit, God gets from us what He wants: worship. If, however, we live after the soul, Satan gets from us what he wants: which is also worship. Many Christians give advantage to Satan. "Blessed are the poor in spirit" (Matt. 5.3a). Those who walk in the spirit and nothing else shall find Satan under their feet. What, then, is worship? "God, I confess I am only a man. I am weak, but You are God."

4 | Worship in Truth

God is a Spirit: and they that worship him must worship in spirit and truth. (John 4.24)

He said, Take now thy son, thine only son, whom thou lovest, even Isaac, and get thee into the land of Moriah; and offer him there for a burnt-offering upon one of the mountains which I will tell thee of. ... And Abraham said unto his young men, Abide ye here with the ass, and I and the lad will go yonder; and we will worship, and come again to you. (Gen. 22.2,5)

Then David arose from the earth, and washed, and anointed himself, and changed his apparel; and he came into the house of Jehovah, and worshipped: then he came to his own house; and when he required, they set bread before him, and he did eat. (2 Sam. 12.20)

We will go into his tabernacles; we will worship at his footstool. (Ps. 132.7)

I will worship toward thy holy temple, and give thanks unto thy name for thy lovingkindness and for thy truth: for thou hast magnified thy word above all thy name. (Ps. 138.2)

We learned earlier that worship of God was adversely influenced by the fall of man. Consequently, if there is no salvation of man, there cannot be Divine worship. Man must be born again.

"The hour cometh, and now is, when the true worshippers shall worship the Father in spirit and truth: for *such* doth the Father seek to be his worshippers" (John 4.23). The Lord Jesus declares that the Father wants *such* to worship. Formerly, He could speak to His people as *God*. But now He speaks to His children as *Father*. "God is a Spirit." It does not say God *has* a Spirit, but God *is* a Spirit. After man's spirit became poisoned through the Fall he could not come to God anymore. He could *feel* and *think* about God, but he could no longer *worship* Him. After the Fall man trusted in reasonings, feelings, thoughts, and decisions.

How can man return to worship God? He who does not know the *Father* cannot worship *God*. The relationship between God and man is a general relationship, but that of the Father and man is an individual one. Because of salvation man can now worship God. It takes the disposition of a son to the Father to know his position as a man and to see the Godhead.

Truth—all that is not out of spirit is not truth. Many use feeling to praise God. This is not truth. Even if we use thoughts to praise God, it is still not truth.

"In Jerusalem is the place where men ought to worship" (John 4.20). Abraham sacrificed his son on Mount Moriah—the site where later the temple was placed in Jerusalem. Many times in the Old Testament it says that worship was on the Mount. In the millennial kingdom all nations will worship in Jerusalem. Why worship in

Jerusalem? Because the temple was there. It is a question of the temple. No temple, no worship. The object of Jerusalem with its temple, altar and other furniture is to teach us that the whole question is of spirit, not of anything else. People forget what these things speak of. What is the position of Jerusalem in God's plan? It represents God's purpose.

In Ephesians 1.18b we read: "the glory of his [God's] inheritance in the saints." What is this inheritance? The glory we can give God, the worship we can give God, the satisfaction we can give God.

Satan does his best to hinder God's people from worship. But we have no other god but God, and we will ask nothing from any other god. God gets glory if we call on His name. Prayer lifts up God.

The *truth* of Jerusalem is spirit. Consider the temple on Mount Moriah. The Lord says, "And I, if I be lifted up from the earth, will draw all men unto myself" (John 12.32). Golgotha at Jerusalem was the place where the Lord was lifted up. Worship and the cross are closely related. If you do not know the cross you cannot worship God. God must touch our natural life. When the cross touches, the man is changed. The backbone of our natural life must be broken. Not only do I *die* with Christ, the death of the Lord *radically wounds* my *self life*. To worship, we must go to the cross. The special character of the cross is to cause us to lose trust in ourselves. The cross makes us *men* once again (and no longer aspiring gods). Unless we take the humble position of man before God we cannot worship.

To illustrate: Once I went to South Fukien to preach, in spite of knowing that God did not want me to go.

Two hundred souls, however, were saved. But later, when I read John 15.5 ("apart from me ye can do nothing"), I found it hard to believe. Finally I received the judgment; for the principle of fallen Eden is: "*I* can, just as God can." We cannot worship with such an attitude. Whenever we feel we have ability we cannot worship.

Let me reiterate: (1) Jerusalem represents God's eternal purpose; (2) Mount Moriah represents the cross dealing with the soul; and (3) the altar of incense represents that all is for God: for "*thine* is the kingdom"—not mine, and not the Devil's: "*thine* is . . . the power"—not mine, nor the Devil's: "*thine* is . . . the glory"—not mine, nor the Devil's. Stand in this position and God will receive worship.

What does the altar of incense mean? As Jesus offered himself to God, so, whenever we tell God we want nothing for ourselves, God gets glory. The incense is to be burned.

In the Old Testament time we had the temple. In the New Testament period the Church, the Body of Christ, is the temple. Hence worship is a corporate matter. In the past, no one could worship outside of the temple, since the temple served as the container of God. Here, then, we see the importance of fellowship. No fellowship, no worship. Fellowship is the basis of worship.

5 | Worship God

The four and twenty elders shall fall down before him that sitteth on the throne, and shall worship him that liveth for ever and ever, and shall cast their crowns before the throne, saying, Worthy art thou, our Lord and our God, to receive the glory and the honor and the power: for thou didst create all things, and because of thy will they were, and were created. (Rev. 4.10–11)

The four living creatures said, Amen. And the elders fell down and worshipped. (Rev. 5.14)

All the angels were standing round about the throne, and about the elders and the four living creatures; and they fell before the throne on their faces, and worshipped God, saying, Amen: Blessing, and glory, and wisdom, and thanksgiving, and honor, and power, and might, be unto our God for ever and ever. Amen. (Rev. 7.11–12)

The four and twenty elders and the four living creatures fell down and worshipped God that sitteth on the throne, saying, Amen; Hallelujah. And a voice came forth from the throne, saying, Give praise to our God, all ye his servants, ye that fear him, the small and the great. And I heard as it were the voice of a great multitude, and as the voice of many waters, and as the voice of mighty thunders, saying, Hallelujah: for the Lord our God, the Almighty, reigneth. (Rev. 19.4–6)

I John am he that heard and saw these things. And when I heard and saw, I fell down to worship before the feet of the angel that showed me these things. And he saith unto me, See thou do it not: I am a fellow-servant with thee and with thy brethren the prophets, and with them that keep the words of this book: worship God. (Rev. 22.8–9)

In the book of Revelation we can draw a line and see what the Devil is fighting for. This book is one of war. The revelation of Christ in its first chapter is a different revelation of Him from what we find in the Gospels. We do not see Him as *the Savior* here in Revelation chapter 1. For John, who once laid his head on His breast, is now lying at the feet of *the Lord* as one dead. We see Him as Lord, as the Lord of war, with His eyes of fire, and out of His mouth a sharp two-edged sword. From chapter 6 on, the Lamb is in wrath. Coming to chapters 11 to 14 we see the Devil using all his strength in war. After chapter 15 and on up to chapter 18, all is war. In chapter 19 we see the greatest fighting of all, for in Revelation it is war between two thrones. Heaven and hell are fighting. And why? To obtain the worship of man.

In Revelation chapters 1–3 we are shown the revelation of Christ as Lord and One who is to be worshipped.

Chapters 4 and 5 are historical, not prophetic, since they do not tell of future days but of the glory of the Creator and the glory of the Redeemer. All beginnings are from the throne. John saw the throne and the One seated there. That One is worthy of *all* praise. The throne has never changed.

Twenty-four elders and four living creatures—the elders are spiritual beings, and the living creatures represent all creation. The twenty-four elders are not part of the Church, since the Biblical number representative of the Church is 12, not 24. They have crowns and thrones. The One Throne is surrounded by twenty-four thrones. If it were possible for the Church to have been enthroned and crowned before the Lamb was, then the twenty-four elders could represent the Church. But that is impossible. The sphere is the universe; consequently, these are the elders of the universe. The Church is only "the brethren of the Lord."

The number 24—David set up twenty-four groups to minister to God (see 1 Chron. 24.3ff.). Here the twenty-four elders form a band who serve God. They are kings, and they are priests. They are angels, a special group of angels who serve God.

On earth men can worship lions, birds and calves, but in heaven these, as represented by the four living creatures, are worshipping God. God rests on His throne; that is the place of our rest too. Men of the world ask: "Where is your God?" And the answer is that He is on His throne, receiving worship.

In Revelation 5, time and history come into view. We saw that the Lamb came. Who can obtain for God what He wants? The Lamb is the only One who came forth. Only He is the One who could restore all to God. According to God, God's throne from eternity to eterniy is in heaven. The earth is in difficulty, for lions, birds and so forth are being worshipped by man. But on the veil of the temple, which typifies the flesh of Christ (see Heb. 10.20), lion and calf and bird and man are all embroidered, for it is said in Exodus 26.31: "thou shalt make a veil of blue, and purple, and scarlet, and fine twined linen: with cherubim the work of the skillful workman shall it be made." And cherubim, we learn from the Scriptures, are the living creatures (see Eze. 10.20). When the veil was rent on the day of Christ's crucifixion (see Matt. 27.51), all that were thus embroidered upon it were also rent. Hence, in His death, Christ redeemed *all creation*. He took us with Him to the cross.

Now the living creatures represent all of God's creation, that is to say, all biological and zoological beings. We are included, and all other living beings are included. From eternity God has His throne, and He receives continual worship. In Biblical zoology we find mentioned not only man but also domestic animals, beasts, birds, fishes and creeping things. Only four are represented here in the four living creatures. Two are missing, as there are no fish and no creeping things. Why? Because creeping things represent the devilish beings, such as the dragon. Fish represent the unsaved, as those who inhabit the sea (which represents the world). There will be no sea in the new heaven and new earth. Accordingly, creatures of the sea are not represented as worshipping God. Nor are the creeping things represented, for they are headed up by the dragon.

The actions of Revelation 4 did not begin when John saw the vision. Because ever since the foundation of the world there has been this worship. On the earth we can have sin, the Devil, and so forth. Earth is the sphere of the Devil's activities now. Finally, the sea will be his sphere as the serpent of the sea. All which happens on the earth does not move the Divine throne at all.

In Revelation 5 we see spiritual creation and physical creation around the throne. There the Lamb stepped forward. We read in Philippians 2.10: "in the name of Jesus every knee should bow, of things in heaven and things on earth and things under the earth." So, here in verse 13 we read: "every created thing which is in the heaven, and on the earth, and under the earth, and on the sea, and all things that are in them, heard I saying, Unto him that sitteth on the throne, and unto the Lamb, be the blessing, and the honor, and the glory, and the dominion, for ever and ever."

In Revelation 4 we find that God receives worship because of *creation*. We see in Revelation 5 that He receives worship because of *redemption*. Here is also the coronation of the Lord Jesus. Chapter 6 to chapter 19 deal mostly with tribulations. And the very last war will be fought between God and Satan.

Why does Satan want the Great Tribulation? Because he wants worship. In chapter 13 we have the beast, the dragon and the image. Satan is not ignorant of what is going to happen to him at the end. Nevertheless, he craves worship so much that he is willing to risk the lake of fire and the bottomless pit to achieve universal worship. He has not had *direct* worship when people have worshipped idols. But during the Great Tribulation men will worship the dragon, which is direct worship. And according to 13.8, "all that dwell on the earth shall worship him"—this is universal worship. Many say today, "I do not worship anything." But at that time they will all worship the beast (see v.12). The Devil uses his own spirit to move men to worship him. From verses 14 and 15 we see that Satan wants men to worship the image of the beast, which in actuality is a worshipping of him himself. He causes all to have the mark of the beast on them. This worship of Satan is the fuller significance of the Great Tribulation.

Chapter 14 tells us what God's reaction to all this will be. Three angels from heaven show the will of God, followed in the early verses of chapter 15 by the victory over the beast.

(1) *The eternal gospel* (vv.6–7). An angel flying in mid-heaven proclaims the eternal gospel, saying, "Fear God, and give him glory; for the hour of his judgment is come: and worship him that made the heaven and the earth and sea and fountains of waters." God stops men from worshipping His enemy.

(2) *The fall of Babylon* (v.8). A second angel announces the fall of Babylon, saying, "Fallen, fallen is Babylon the great, that hath made all the nations to drink of the wine of the wrath of her fornication."

(3) *The wrath of God* (vv.9–10). The third angel declares that the wrath of God is come and that there is no more grace: "If any man worshippeth the beast and his image, and receiveth a mark on his forehead, or upon his hand, he also shall drink of the wine of the wrath of God, which is prepared unmixed in the cup of his anger; and he shall be tormented with fire

and brimstone in the presence of the holy angels and in the presence of the Lamb."

In the same chapter we see how God will separate men. The difference is whether or not men have worshipped Satan or God.

(4) *Victory over the beast* (15.2-4). Salvation is our portion, the human portion. Worship is the Divine portion.

In chapter 16 we see how wrath shall be poured out on the unsaved. Verses 1 and 2 tell us that judgment will come on the worshippers of the beast. Sadly, however, men will not repent but shall blaspheme God instead (vv.9,11,21).

Chapter 19 follows chapter 16. In verse 4 we see that the four and twenty elders and the four living creatures worship God. In verse 5 the call to God's servants is to give praise to Him. In verse 6 there is mentioned the voice of a great multitude, saying, "Hallelujah: for the Lord our God, the Almighty, reigneth." It is not improper *not* to mention salvation when praising God.

In verse 20 we learn that the beast shall be totally destroyed: "the beast was taken, and with him the false prophet that wrought the signs in his sight, wherewith he deceived them that had received the mark of the beast and them that worshipped his image: they two were cast alive into the lake of fire that burneth with brimstone."

Chapter 20.4—the thrones are set and judgment given. The issue of the kingdom revolves around the question of men worshipping Satan or God.

Chapters 21 and 22 relate to eternity. In verses 1-3 of chapter 21 we see that the tabernacle of God is with men, who shall be His "peoples." This speaks of their relation to God, who shall be their God. God's portion is secured among men.

"He that overcometh shall inherit these things; and I will be his God, and he shall be my son" (v.7). To know Him as God, one must first know him as Father. The highest knowledge of God is not Fatherhood but Godhood. He who overcomes overcomes the world (see 1 John 5.4–5).

In chapter 22 we find that John wants to worship the angel (vv.8–9). Our tendency to worship something less than God is deeply inbred in us. The angel provides the proper antidote for such a tendency: "worship God" is the last command.

In worship I acknowledge my limitations. In worship I also acknowledge that God has no limitations. I bow before Him. He is beyond me in everything.

6 | Worship the Ways of God

The man bowed his head, and worshipped Jehovah.
... And it came to pass, that, when Abraham's servant
heard their words, he bowed himself down to the earth
unto Jehovah. (Gen. 24.26,52)

Aaron spake all the words which Jehovah had spoken
unto Moses, and did the signs in the sight of the people.
And the people believed: and when they heard that
Jehovah had visited the children of Israel, and that he had
seen their affliction, then they bowed their heads and worshipped. (Ex. 4.30–31)

Ye shall say, It is the sacrifice of Jehovah's passover,
who passed over the houses of the children of Israel in
Egypt, when he smote the Egyptians, and delivered our
houses. And the people bowed the head and worshipped.
(Ex. 12.27)

Jehovah descended in the cloud, and stood with him
there, and proclaimed the name of Jehovah. And Jehovah
passed by before him, and proclaimed, Jehovah, Jehovah,
a God merciful and gracious, slow to anger, and abun-

dant in lovingkindness and truth; keeping lovingkindness for thousands, forgiving iniquity and transgression and sin; and that will by no means clear the guilty, visiting the iniquity of the fathers upon the children, and upon the children's children, upon the third and upon the fourth generation. And Moses made haste, and bowed his head toward the earth, and worshipped. And he said, If now I have found favor in thy sight, O Lord, let the Lord, I pray thee, go in the midst of us; for it is a stiffnecked people; and pardon our iniquity and our sin, and take us for thine inheritance. (Ex. 34.5–9)

He said, Nay; but as prince of the host of Jehovah am I now come. And Joshua fell on his face to the earth, and did worship, and said unto him, What saith my Lord unto his servant? (Joshua 5.14)

It was so, when Gideon heard the telling of the dream, and the interpretation thereof, that he worshipped; and he returned into the camp of Israel, and said, Arise; for Jehovah hath delivered into your hand the host of Midian. (Judges 7.15)

For this child I prayed; and Jehovah hath given me my petition which I asked of him: therefore also I have granted him to Jehovah; as long as he liveth he is granted to Jehovah. And he worshipped Jehovah there. (1 Sam. 1.27–28)

It came to pass on the seventh day, that the child died. And the servants of David feared to tell him that the child was dead; for they said, Behold, while the child was yet alive, we spake unto him, and he hearkened not unto our voice: how will he then vex himself, if we tell him that the child is dead! But when David saw that his servants were whispering together, David perceived that the child was dead; and David said unto his servants, Is the child dead? And they said, He is dead. Then David arose from the earth, and washed, and anointed himself, and changed his apparel; and he came into the house of Jehovah, and worshipped: then he came to his own house; and when he required, they set bread before him, and he did eat. (2 Sam. 12.18–20)

Then Job arose, and rent his robe, and shaved his head, and fell down upon the ground, and worshipped. (Job 1.20)

It is impossible to only worship God, for the knowledge of God leads to the acceptance of His ways. On the one hand we want to know God. On the other hand we want to know His ways. And hence, we not only must worship God, we also must worship His ways.

By revelation we know God; by surrender we know His ways. No man can choose his own way. God decides His own ways of dealing with us. First, it is necessary for us to have revelation that we may see God's ways, since God works according to His pleasure. "I worship You, and I worship Your ways." True worship comes from revelation. If you cannot learn to worship God's ways, you will have no future in spiritual affairs. What are God's ways? That which God does in me, that is, in my body.

We read in Genesis 24 that Abraham's servant had a difficult task. On the road he looked to God. When he came to the well of water outside the city of Nahor, he prayed. Rebekah came and did exactly what he had prayed for. So the servant worshipped God's ways. Worship is giving glory to God. The worship I give God is His glory. We cannot glorify God in any greater fashion than by worship. The proud cannot worship. "Fortunately, I did a thing well," the proud one says. He obviously has not seen God yet.

Now after Abraham's servant came into the house and told his business to Laban and Bethuel, he immediately worshipped God when he received an affirmative answer. He did not say thank you to Laban, he instead thanked God, because the servant recognized that all had come out of God. The more we worship, the more opportunities we will have to worship.

In Exodus 4 it is told that the children of Israel heard that God had seen their affliction. They bowed their heads and worshipped Him. Sometimes God leads us in specific actions as He had led Abraham's servant. In the case of Israel, however, He had not yet *done* anything. He only saw their affliction and remembered His covenant. Nevertheless, when the children of Israel learned that God had remembered, that was enough: they immediately worshipped.

Should we ever say, "God has forgotten," then we cannot worship.

Exodus 12 tells of God instructing His people how to answer their children whenever they should ask the meaning of the Passover. To keep the Passover is to remember God's ways. God destroyed the Egyptians and "passed over" Israel. So, the people worshipped. When we see the difference between ourselves and the world, as typified by the Egyptians, we will worship. Moses did not tell the people to worship, but because they saw God's ways they automatically worshipped.

In Exodus 32 is the story of how, while Moses was up on the Sinai mount to receive the Ten Commandments, the people below worshipped the golden calf — another god. This provoked God to great displeasure, and Moses pleaded with God for them. After he went down to deal with the situation on the plain, Moses ascended the mount a second time. "And Jehovah passed by before him, and proclaimed, Jehovah, Jehovah, a God merciful and gracious, slow to anger, and abundant in lovingkindness and truth; keeping lovingkindness for thousands, forgiving iniquity and transgression and sin" (vv.6–7a). It would not have been surprising if at this point Moses had worshipped. But it was *at the end of the second part* of verse 7 that "Moses made haste, and bowed down his head toward the earth, and worshipped" (v.8). This second part was totally different from the first: the first part spoke of God's mercy and grace and forgiveness, whereas in the second part the Lord is recorded as declaring: "and that will by no means clear the guilty, visiting the iniquity of the fathers upon the children, and upon the children's children, upon the third and upon the fourth generation." This spoke of the imposing majesty of God, to which Moses made haste to worship. Hence, it is not just a matter of our knowing God's grace, but our also knowing His holiness. Both are reflected in His ways — and *all* God's ways are to be worshipped.

I love verses 9 and 8. In verse 9 Moses prayed, but in verse 8 he worshipped. First worship, then prayer. Worship represents what God wants, and prayer represents what I want. Christians have a lesson to learn, which is, to learn to appreciate the ways of God. Learn to take pleasure in God's ways and in His pleasure.

In the book of Joshua we see that God commissioned Joshua to lead the children of Israel into Canaan. Moses and Aaron were by this time both gone from the scene. The young man Joshua was left alone. This responsibility now upon him was truly awesome and heavy. How would he feel at this time? At that point he was given a vision. He saw a big man with a sword drawn in his hand. Not knowing who this man was, he asked, "Art thou for us, or for our adversaries?" (5.13) The man did not say, "I am come to help you"; instead, he said "No" to both questions: "Nay; but as prince of the host of Jehovah am I now come" (5.14a). From this incident we must see that it is not a question of Divine help but of whether or not we are willing to do His will. Joshua, for one, was willing: "And Joshua fell on his face to the earth, and did worship" (v.14b). It is not a question of God's help but one of bowing to His leadership. If we know this part of the ways of God—that is to say, that God wants to be the Captain and to do all things—we will worship!

In the seventh chapter of Judges we learn that Gideon was uncertain of victory or defeat. He ventured into the camp of the Midianites and heard one of them telling a dream to another: "Behold, I dreamed a dream; and, lo, a cake of barley bread tumbled into the camp of Midian, and came unto the tent, and smote it so that it fell, and turned it upside down, so that the tent lay flat. And his fellow answered and said, This is nothing else save the sword of Gideon the son of Joash, a man of Israel; into his hand God hath delivered Midian, and all the host" (vv.13b–14). When Gideon heard the telling of the dream and its interpretation, "he worshipped" (v.15). And why? He worshipped not only God himself but also what God would do: he not only worshipped the power of God but also worshipped the *way* He would accomplish His purpose. The portion which God should obtain from His people is that of worship. This does not mean that His work is not important; it simply means that worship glorifies God.

It is clear in 1 Samuel 1 that Hannah touched the spirit of worship. She prayed for a son, and God gave her a son. After Hannah weaned him she brought him to Shiloh to the house of Jehovah. There she confessed: "For this child I prayed; and Jehovah hath given me my petition which I asked of him: therefore also I have granted him to Jehovah; as long as he liveth he is granted to Jehovah" (vv.27-28). Only this kind of person can worship God. Hannah worshipped Jehovah. Those who do not stop at God's gifts but who also seek His face are those who can truly worship. One who is not surrendered to God cannot worship.

I often find the words which Abraham spoke to his servants as they approached Mount Moriah to be most precious: "I and the lad will go yonder; and we will worship, and come again to you" (Gen. 22.5b). Worship is to offer Isaac to God. I do not believe that one can truly worship without true consecration. When we give our Samuel or our Isaac to God, worship will follow, for worship follows the altar—the cross. Where there is the cross, altar and surrender, there is worship.

God's ways are not always demonstrated in His hearing our prayers. Sometimes God does not answer prayer. In 2 Samuel 11 and 12 we find recorded the story of David's sin with Bathsheba, and of how the child that was born became sick. Although God had said that the child would die, David nevertheless prayed that he might be healed. He prayed earnestly, but the child died. Unlike David, many who do not bow to God's will will have controversy with God. But David, when he heard that the child had died, washed and entered the temple and worshipped.

What is worship? "I bow under the ways of God." *That* is worship. Many times God has to vindicate himself in His holiness and righteousness. Because we fall and sin, God's governmental hand must show itself plainly so that all may know that He has no part in our sin. No man can worship if he does not humbly bow beneath God's hand. Without submission to God we cannot worship His ways. "I adore Thy ways."

Finally, it should be noted that Job, being a perfect and an upright man, was one day suddenly stripped of *everything*. Everything was gone, even all his children. "Then Job arose, and rent his robe, and shaved his head, and fell down upon the ground, and worshipped; and he said, Naked came I out of my mother's womb, and naked shall I return thither: Jehovah gave, and Jehovah hath taken away; blessed be the name of Jehovah" (Job 1.20–21). This was the very first thing Job did. He not only worshipped God for God himself, he also worshipped God for His ways. Here was a case where there was no vindication of God's holiness in view. It simply pleased God to do this to His servant. And Job's reaction was: he bowed under the ways of God. There is no worship better than this of Job's. Let us therefore worship God under whatever circumstances He may allow.

PART TWO

MORE FROM THE MINISTRY OF 1939-40*

*Being a reproduction of further notes—taken down in English by a dear Christian sister now with the Lord—of some of the author's other messages delivered in Chinese during this period, with, as before, no more than some necessary tidying up added.—*Editor*

1 | Notes on Conflict or Battle

One*

Do you know that there is a war going on? If you say "No," I do not believe it. Yet if you should say that you know, I must confess to you that it does not look like it. This matter is not taken seriously enough by God's people. We ought to have a fighting note about us. Instead, we fail to see clearly that during these past two thousand years, though Satan may not have been ruling, he certainly has been resisting.

According to God's thought the Church has been placed on a war-footing. Everything ought to be in relation to this. If the Church is not a militant Church, it is not a Church at all. For God only recognizes a militant Church. If we are still bound by the earth, by ourselves or by the Devil, it is because we do not see our Enemy. Let it be known that we have three enemies:

---

*The material found in this first subsection was delivered by the author at a workers' meeting. — *Editor* the world, the flesh and the Devil. Just as our God is a Triune God, so our Enemy is also three-in-one.

How do we recognize the Enemy? Which one do we first overcome—the world, the flesh or the Devil? (1) According to experience, *the world* is the first to be overcome. This is the lowest plane of victory. If we are touched by the spirit of the world in our life and work, then we are out of the battle. In order to be overcomers, what we must overcome is not only the *things* of the world but also the *spirit* of the world. In overcoming the world we maintain our proper relationship with the Father.

(2) *The flesh.* The world is outward, but Satan has planted something *in* us. You can have a clear break with the world, but you will find that there is something following you everywhere. You cannot get away from it. In the very best thing you do, you will find that you yourself are in everything. God has to take many years to deal with us till He can show us *ourselves* in His light, and then we shall be properly weakened. Light results in the flesh not being able to rise up in the same way as before, because now it has no strength left. Only after this dealing can we know the third enemy, Satan.

(3) *The Devil.* Because he is a spirit, only those who have been set free from the flesh can—in their spirit—know the battle in the spirit realm. Those who are in the flesh only know what the flesh is. Hence all who have not been delivered from the world and the flesh are fuzzy towards Satan. In the Letter to the Ephesians we find that it is only in the sixth and final chapter that warfare is mentioned. Just as explained in the earlier

chapters of Ephesians, the first two issues — the world and the flesh — have to be solved in our lives before we get to the third — the Devil.

If we do not sense the battle, there is no need to discuss being overcomers. Overcomers are not those who have a little more spirituality than other believers. Being good will not make you an overcomer. Yet obviously, if our personal life is not right, we will be full of problems. We should be crying to God night and day for deliverance from such problems.

There is nothing said in the relevant Scripture passage about the *life* of the "man child" (see Rev. 12). For him there is but one objective — the Enemy. We often ask about this or that, this person or that person, and so forth. But about the "man child" only one thing is mentioned, for there are far greater issues at stake than our own personal problems.

I would love to tell everyone that the kingdom of God is near. If you truly saw the kingdom, then the fighting note would never be absent from you. To sing the battle song in time of peace and in time of war are two, very different things.

There was a war going on in the universe even before what we find in Genesis. May God keep our spirit strong. The world and the flesh may very easily make an impression on your spirit. If that is all, you are dimmed. Spiritual facts will become mere doctrine, not life; they will become mere words. I do fervently hope that we may be able to live as though there is a battle going on.

Once a lady asked me to supper. She said, "I do not have any good food. Wait till the war is over." Such is truly a war-footing attitude.

Two—More Notes on Conflict or Warfare*

If we are ruled by the world, if we are ruled by self, if we are ruled by circumstances, if we are ruled by man, or if we are ruled by earth, we are unfit for warfare.

The age between twenty and sixty is most valuable: "thy estimation shall be of the male from twenty years old even unto sixty years old, even thy estimation shall be fifty shekels of silver, after the shekel of the sanctuary" (Lev. 27.3). This is the highest estimation paid concerning all ages. And why? Because it is said in Numbers: "from twenty years old and upward, all that are able *to go forth to war*" (1.3). In other words, God's highest estimate of a man's value is his ability to engage in warfare.

To be a part of the man-child company, we must have an utter consecration, a higher and deeper consecration. An ordinary consecration—such as that which takes place just after we are saved—will not do. We must have a consecration that demands our very life.

We must have ascension life. If we live an earthly life, we cannot be in that company of overcomers. I often say in God's presence, "I am the poorest, but I am in the presence of the Richest." If you come to God and have nothing to ask, it is either because you are not poor enough or you do not know how rich God is.

If you are not a warrior you are of no governmental use to God. Particularly since the turn of the present century the Church has come to know something of the recovery of spiritual warfare; yet much, if not

---

*These further words on the subject were delivered by the author at another workers' meeting.—*Editor*

all about it is in the personal realm. But we are told by the Lord: "upon this rock I will build my church; and the gates of Hades shall not prevail against it" (Matt. 16.18). It is against the Church that the gates of Hades shall not prevail. The passage reads, "shall not prevail against *it*," not "against them."

The "man child" (Rev. 12) is a body, not a member. The woman is still the Jerusalem above. In that day, that is, in the day when the New Jerusalem shall descend from heaven, no "man child company" will be seen.

We are plainly told who the dragon is. That the man child shall rule with an iron rod shows clearly who the man child is. But we are not told in Revelation 12 who the woman is. All is in symbolic language. The Church is to be on a wartime footing. To maintain a fighting note is indeed a most difficult task. It is so easy to let warfare get lost in service. If only the Church in China were a truly fighting church!!! The cry of war is not strong enough!

An overcomer must know the *life* of the Body of Christ. It is not enough to know only the *principles* of the Body.

In the seven letters to the seven churches, from the church at Ephesus to the church at Laodicea, there is one constant note sounded—that of overcoming, that of warfare. Ephesians 2 speaks of the heavenlies, but so does Ephesians 6. The whole armor of God is Christ: He is the girdle of truth, the breastplate of righteousness, and so forth. However, it is not the Armor that fights; it is the Body who fights. Yet the Armor and the Body are one.

It is strange that we often say, "Ye must be born again in order to enter the house of God"; but God says we must be born again in order to enter *the kingdom*.

We all remember Nehemiah who wrought greatly in the work of building the wall of Jerusalem with one hand but also fought against the enemies with the other hand (see Neh. 4.15-23).

You can never truly know spiritual warfare until you are in the heavenlies. If you are bound to the earth, you may know warfare, but it will only touch the realm of the flesh. Ephesians 1-2 shows what our position is. Ephesians 6 shows that our foes are in the heavenlies. This is why we need to be seated *there*. The intervening chapters say nothing of the heavenlies (except in 3.10).

In Leviticus we find worship—*my* position, *my* sacrifice, all of it personal. But as soon as we read our way into Numbers, we are plunged into warfare. God's estimate of a man's value is his ability to war. As a matter of fact, we find war from the beginning to the end of the Old Testament. God's people always warred. At times God even allowed enemies to come lest His people might forget how to war.

Everything depends on our reaction when we hear of the eternal purpose of God. We read in Revelation 1.9: "I John, your brother and partaker with you in the tribulation and kingdom and patience which are in Jesus, was in the isle that is called Patmos, for the word of God and the testimony of Jesus." John said he was a partaker in tribulation. Why did he say he was also a partaker in the patience of Jesus? Here is an important matter. Much of the word in Revelation is that of wrath and judgment. We share in the tribulation now, and we shall share in the kingdom of the future. God desires us to touch His judgments. If we do so, we are assured of a part in His patience. Judgment is certain; if it were not so, there would be no need of patience. Yet, when the Lord finally lays aside His patience, that will be the signal that judgment will fall. This is the time of His patience; hence, we can have part in His patience.

2 | The Offence of the Lord

On one occasion, involving John the Baptist, the Lord said: "blessed is he, whosoever shall find no occasion of stumbling in me" (Matt. 11.6). In Darby's version it reads: "blessed is whosoever shall not be offended in me." What does this mean? It means that we do not like what the Lord does. And from our perspective we have good reason for not liking it. In our own eyes we ought to be offended. *That* is the offence of the Lord. What the Lord did or did not do caused John the Baptist to be offended. John was not offended by the Pharisees or the publicans, but by the Lord. And from his standpoint he had reason to be offended.

Why was he offended? He had hoped that Israel would be restored as a nation—that the kingdom would be re-established in justice and righteousness. He had hoped the Lord would bring in a revival. The first Elijah had gone up to Mount Carmel and had wrought mightily. Israel was revived and Elijah's ministry vindicated. But the second Elijah, John the Baptist (see

Matt. 17.9–13), was put into prison and was soon to
be killed, and yet no national restoration was in sight.
So John sent a message to the Lord, because he was
greatly offended. He thought, if *I* am not to accomplish
anything, then surely *You*, Lord, are to do so! *You* ought
to do something! Couched in a sting of rebuke, John's
message to Jesus was: "Art thou he that cometh, or look
we for another?" (Matt. 11.3) He wanted something
done by the Lord by which to demonstrate who he,
John, was. From John's viewpoint, nothing had been
done thus far by Jesus to show who he indeed was, and
thus nothing done by which to vindicate his ministry
which had now by his imprisonment come to an end.

To "not be offended in me" is not to be offended
by what the Lord does or does not do. We feel the Lord
does not do what we want, what we feel He ought to
do—that He does not vindicate us. Are we pleased with
the *way* of the Lord with us? This is not just a matter
of knowing and doing God's will, but a matter of
whether or not we *like His ways*. Often we *can* do God's
will, even though we may do it weeping; even so, we
are offended by the way He does things. We are offended with His way, His road, His method, and so forth.
And thus it would seem as if we have a legitimate reason
to be displeased.

This has nothing to do with our Lord's dealings with
our flesh, our sacrifice, and so on. For such dealings
are on a far lower plane. But I am here speaking of those
who have been brought to a place where the *whole* heart
is for God, such as was the case with John the Baptist.
We have sought to know His will; we have sought
nothing for ourselves; we only want glory for God

alone; and yet, in many of God's ways with us, we are disappointed. For example, we have come to a great difficulty, and yet no way through is opened up; we are ill and expect Him to heal us, and yet we are not healed; we are weak, and yet no strength is given; we are short of money, and yet no money comes. It seems as if God does not measure up to our expectations of Him. When such happens again and again, this is what we call "the offence of the Lord." Many people lack the qualifications to be offended by the Lord. On the contrary, their fall is because of the flesh and the world. When the Lord seems to disappoint them it is *they* who have been wrong, and they know and ultimately acknowledge it.

Not to be offended in the Lord is the highest and deepest form of discipline. Often we feel the Lord *must* come in because of His testimony, because His honor and His faithfulness are at stake; yet He does *not* come in. God led the children of Israel out of Egypt, and then they were pursued. They got to a place where they were shut in by the enemy from behind, mountains were to the right and left, and the Red Sea was in front. But then God opened a way through the sea. So whenever we too get to the place where we are shut in, we always expect God to open a way through for us; yet often He does not do so: the prison gates do not open, the money does not come, the situation is not dealt with. Nevertheless, just here lies the test. Those who love the ways of the Lord can look up and say, "You were not pleased for us to die in Egypt, but You are pleased for us to die near the Red Sea. Whether the Red Sea opens or not we are content, we are glad."

Madame Guyon once said, "I believe God more than

His word." Even though God does not seem to keep His promise, we believe Him in spite of that. Now *this* is to not be offended in the Lord.

When there has been an utter consecration, more than when we are saved, more than when we give ourselves to His service—when there is a mighty consecration, an awesome devotion to Him—it is when we get to *that* place, that *then* we expect God to do something for us. If we have such an utterness towards the Lord, then we have a great expectancy. (If, of course, we have not got to that stage, we can explain away much of everything which happens to us on the ground of our *own* weakness—that it is because *we* were wrong or mistaken, etc., etc.) But if we get to that place of utterness with the Lord just now described wherein we expect to see God's deliverance and yet He does not come in, wherein we feel we have a *right* for God to do such and such and He does not do it—*that* is the offence of the Lord of which we have been speaking. Yet it is those who are not offended who are blessed. We need, therefore, to get to a point where we have a liking *for His ways*, where we can say: "If You, Lord, (I state it reverently here) act according to Your promise, good; but if not, it is also good."

There will indeed come a day when all things shall be explained and we shall *see* that God was right. At the present moment, however, His ways are much higher than our ways, and so we at times cannot see and understand. But when we stand before the judgment seat, not only will it be the occasion at which we shall be judged, it will also be the occasion at which God (again, I reverently state it) will have to explain things to us.

There will be many cases in which I thought I was right but I was wrong, yet there will also be other cases about which God will say, "I was right, but you were right also."

3 | A Root Out of a Dry Ground

> He grew up before him as a tender plant, and as a root
> out of a dry ground: he hath no form nor comeliness;
> and when we see him, there is no beauty that we should
> desire him. (Is. 53.2)
>
> Then began he to upbraid the cities wherein most of
> his mighty works were done, because they repented not.
> ... At that season Jesus answered and said, I thank thee,
> O Father, Lord of heaven and earth, that thou didst hide
> these things from the wise and understanding, and didst
> reveal them unto babes. (Matt. 11.20,25)

"Then" and "at that season." What was the time or
season referred to in the passage in Matthew? It was
the time when the cities had not repented (see vv.20–21)
and when the Lord had upbraided them because of the
hardness of their hearts. It was just at that time when
the Lord answered and said, "I thank thee, O Father,
Lord of heaven and earth." In Luke's account (10.21)

we read: "In that same hour he rejoiced in the Holy Spirit." At that moment He was filled with joy in the Holy Spirit.

"A root out of a dry ground." What does it mean to be a root out of a *dry* ground? The root is the channel for deriving life, the instrument by which the plant is fed, nourished, given life. A root out of a dry ground means that there was no supply from circumstances, that the Lord found nothing on earth or from man to give life and to supply nourishment. If the Lord were to derive His life from circumstances He could not have gone on, for it seemed as if all was an utter failure. And yet it was *just at that time* that He rejoiced in spirit. The situation had been brought home to Him, and He had found it necessary to pronounce woes upon the various cities because of their unbelief, and yet at that very moment He offered up praise. What for? He praised the Father for His ways, for His will. He delighted in the will of the Father—whatever it was. We may reluctantly be doing the will of God, but it is quite a different thing to *love* God's will and ways. The Lord rejoiced in the Holy Spirit because of the ways of God. Even when He was going to the cross He could say to His disciples: "my peace I give unto you" (John 14.27a). Here, in spite of apparent failure, He was filled with joy because this was the will of the Father. It is a great thing to be able to say, "Lord, I love Thy ways."

"A root out of a dry ground." This means no support or encouragement from outward circumstances. On the one hand we must be prepared to lose our individualism, for we are not to be free lances, and the Church, the Body of Christ, is to be protection and strength for us. But on the other hand we are to live a life in which we are prepared to have nothing even from our brethren. Paul once declared: "all that are in Asia turned away from me" (2 Tim. 1.15a). So we have to be prepared to receive no support from the brethren, for we cannot in all situations exact Body help from them. We must not, as it were, go off on a tangent. We have to accept the limitations of the Body, and yet, at the same time, we have to find all our resources in God. All eagles fly alone. There is a loneliness of life, a loneliness of spirit, which we have to go through if we are to press on with God.

To be a root out of a dry ground means that nothing circumstantial will move us. Romans 8.37 states that "in all these things we are more than conquerors through him that loved us." Paul did not say "above" or "out of" all things, but *in* the very midst of them all. And so it means that no support is offered to us by our circumstances to lead us on with God, that there is nothing coming to us from outside, that there is only one supply or source of life. In some situations, even our brethren cannot be the ones to supply us with life. We have only one source of life, and we must not look to any other. Life is given by God. I go on with Him. Life in God is deeper even than prayer, witnessing or Bible study. There is indeed meat in doing the will of God (see John 4.34). But there is life and sustenance even deeper than this. Sometimes in doing the will of God there is darkness and not light, for the word of God strikes hard; and then we have to just live by the *life of God;* for there is nothing from outside to minister to us.

When we are successful there is joy, and when we

are unsuccessful we are apt to be cast down. But a root
out of a dry ground means that our joy, our life, does
not come from outside. From where do we derive our
life? We must get to the place where all we have is in
God alone, otherwise we shall get held up by things and
even people who are the Lord's. We have to come to
the place of "God, my exceeding joy." If we are deriving our joy from circumstances, then we will be long-
ing to go on furlough, or do this or that! If the root
is drawing life from circumstances, then we will have
nothing with which to go on.

We are to live *by* the Father to be the root out of
a dry ground even though we would never naturally
choose it. We will find we have to be cast on God and
on Him alone. Our brethren cannot come in where we
look for most; we will be most disappointed. We have
to learn to have one joy only, joy in the Holy Spirit.
It is a great thing to learn to be shut up to God and
to live by Him alone. Even if earth *is* supplying you
with something—whether the assembly, your fellow-
workers, or whatever—take all these sparingly. Otherwise, someday you will feel cast down if you cannot
have them. True, I live with my fellow-members of the
Body, but I do not live *by* them. If we learn this we
shall go on steadily. We live by the Father. Jesus rejoiced
in God.

4 | What Is Necessary for Revelation

Two things are necessary for revelation: (1) light from God, and (2) opened eyes.

The reason why many do not see is not because there is no light. The difficulty is that our eyes are blind, not that God is withholding light. Lack of revelation is due to blind eyes. We think we are all right. We think we know and understand. Hence, it is no wonder that we get no light.

In very identical circumstances some people will see more and others less because their inward eyes are not the same. Those who are not conscious of need or think that there is not much wrong suffer loss as a consequence.

The Lord talked of a pit, blind men, and leaders of the blind (see Matt. 15.14). Here are three factors. If there were no pit, it would not matter whether we were blind or not; but there *is* a pit, and consequently, they who are blind will fall into it.

There are three different forms of blindness:

(1) Those who are built up by all they have heard. "Yes, I see that. I saw it at such and such a time." "Yes, I have known that for years." They have never really seen, yet they are confirmed in their blindness by what they have heard.

(2) Those who oppose everything.

(3) Those who agree easily with everything you say but are not exercised by it. So they get nowhere.

The *only* condition (and I say it again and again, and cannot say it strongly enough), the only condition for seeing is the cross. We go round and round in our own thoughts, wisdom and ideas; but human wisdom has no part at all in spiritual things. It does not enter in; it is entirely excluded. It is the cross that makes us see. When the cross operates we see. The cross is not a doctrine but an experience. It is possible to talk much about the doctrine of the cross and to know a lot about it in our heads and yet for the cross never to have touched our lives. Some of us are humble because we are in darkness. Yet our humility is from ourselves and is simply dead works. We hear humility spoken of, and so we produce a humility. Instead of seeing, instead of having light and being dealt with by the cross, we think we have to *do* something about it.

In the Scriptures we read of many who met God and were cast down. They were struck down by the light of God and were done for. But there are many today who throw themselves down instead of being cast down by the light. They act it out. They produce something which has not come from God. If God indeed meets with us, if His light slays us, it is something quite apart from ourselves, and the time and circumstances are not under our control. There are some who seek to *produce* something, who try to do it themselves; they choose the way and the time and place. It is all useless, however, and absolutely of no value. This all has to be got rid of before God can do anything.

If we have once had a fundamental seeing, then we will *go on* seeing. There will be an open heaven.

There are those who have *too* many experiences, and they are only built up by them all. We do not need *many* experiences; we need *great* experiences, something drastic and fundamental. Some of us think we have been dealt with so often; in fact, we are always being dealt with. As a result, we think we are all right; yet these many dealings only nourish our pride. Those who have been dealt with most in small ways (that is, without having the fundamental dealings first) are the most proud. If we lack the fundamental dealings of the natural life, nothing else is of any use. Only those who have had that fundamental blow can cease from their own works.

There are those who cast themselves down, humble themselves, but it is only a kind of daily drill. They try to act out what they have heard, but it has absolutely no spiritual value. It cannot do anything for them, apart from making them proud.

We cannot use our own strength to produce anything of spiritual value. A daily seeing comes from a fundamental opening of our eyes.

When and how God will strike us down, we do not know; but, if we are living before Him with an *honest* heart and are handed over to Him and have put ourselves in His hands, He will bring it about. He will do it.

"The eyes of Jehovah run to and fro throughout the whole earth, to show himself strong in the behalf of them whose heart is perfect toward him" (2 Chron. 16.9a). A perfect heart is an honest heart. God is not afraid of those who kick against the goads. Saul kicked, but he was honest. God is only afraid of actors.

All spiritual experiences come from inward seeing. We can have no real experience apart from seeing. It is fatal for many people to hear anything because they immediately try to act it out. Some of God's servants groan because so many hear and do not do; I, on the contrary, am more afraid of those who hear and *do,* because for many it is only dead works: they are acting it out; they are trying to produce it. It is not we who have to produce anything; it is God who does it. An unsaved man who tries to act as a saved man only delays matters, for in his case he had two steps to take instead of one. He had first to *stop* doing the one before he could be taken into the other.

There was a man of whom it was said, "He is at present unnatural. We will have to wait until he has got rid of all that before we can see whether God will be able to do anything for him or not. He has first to get rid of that which is only put on."

5 | Spiritual Reality

Spiritual reality has this outstanding characteristic, that it bears no mark of time. The time factor vanishes the instant you touch that reality. From the human point of view there is such a thing as prophecy, but from the Divine viewpoint no such thing exists. "Thou art my son; this day have I begotten thee" (Ps. 2.7). With God it is always "this day." Our Lord says, "I am the Alpha and the Omega, the first and the last, the beginning and the end" (Rev. 22.13). He is both together, both at once. It is not that at one time He is first and at another time He is last. He is first and last simultaneously. Nor is it that having been Alpha for some time, He becomes Omega later on. To the contrary, He is Alpha and Omega from eternity to eternity. He is always first *and* last; and He is always Alpha *and* Omega. In the sight of man He is not Omega till He is manifested as Omega; but in the sight of God He is Omega now. With man, the past and the future are separate; with God they synchronize. The "I" of yesterday differs from the "I" of today; and the "I" of tomorrow differs further still. But "Jesus Christ is the same yesterday, and today, yea and for ever" (Heb. 13.8). God is the eternal "I Am." It is here that the knowledge of God comes in.

Our Lord once said, "No one hath ascended into heaven, but he that descended out of heaven, even the Son of man, who is in heaven" (John 3.13). Note how these two different positions synchronize in Christ. There is no change of time or place with Him. Of God it is written: "the Father of lights, with whom can be no variation, neither shadow that is cast by turning" (James 1.17). He is that himself: He is that in His Christ: He is that in His Church.

Have you ever come across the Church that Paul describes in 1 Corinthians 6.11? "But ye were washed, but ye were sanctified, but ye were justified in the name of the Lord Jesus Christ, and in the Spirit of our God." You say, "Oh, that describes the *position* of the Church." No, it describes the *reality* of the Church. Paul, in writing to the Romans, was more daring than some who later translated his writings. In referring to the believers at Rome, he wrote that they were "called saints" or "saints by calling" (Rom. 1.7). Later translators thought it was running too great a risk to translate this literally, and so they safeguarded their own conception of spiritual things by writing that the Roman believers were "called *to be* saints." If we are only called *to be* saints, how long shall we have to be being before we can actually be? Praise God, we *are* saints! The statement translated as "we are his workmanship" (Eph. 2.10) would be more accurately rendered as "we are his masterpiece." The Church is the very best God can pro-

duce. It can never be improved upon. Once we have seen
the spiritual reality of the Church, we shall never hope
for any progress. There is no scope whatever for progress in the Church, for the Church is already God's
masterpiece.

We look around and see breakdown everywhere. We
wonder to ourselves: "What is the Church coming to?"
Yet, she is not "coming to"; she has arrived. We do not
look forward to discover the goal, we look back. God
reached His end in Christ before the foundation of the
world (see Eph. 1.4). We move forward on the basis of
what already is; and as we move forward on the basis
of God's eternal facts, we shall see the manifestation
of those facts. We are not waiting until His purpose —
His eternal purpose — becomes a fact; we are only
waiting for the manifestation of the fact.

Spiritual progress is not a question of attaining to
some abstract standard, not a question of pressing
through to some far-off goal; it is wholly a question
of seeing *God's* standard. Spiritual progress comes by
finding out what you really are, not by trying to be what
you hope to be. You will never reach that goal, however
earnestly you strive. It is when you *see* you are dead
that you die; it is when you *see* you are risen that you
rise; it is when you *see* you are holy that you become
holy. It is *seeing* the goal that determines the *pathway*
to the goal. The goal is revealed by inward seeing, not
by desiring or by working. There is only one possibility
of spiritual progress, and that is by discovering God's
facts. Our great need is just to *see* the truth as *God*
sees it — the truth concerning Christ, the truth concerning ourselves in Christ, and the truth concerning the
Church, the Body of Christ.

In Romans 8.30 Paul wrote: "whom he [God] foreordained, them he also called: and whom he called, them he also justified: and whom he justified, them he also glorified." Accordingly to God's word, all who are called have already been glorified. The goal is attained! The Church has already come to glory! None who see the spiritual reality of the Church would ever say that that is merely positional. It is real, and anything else is false. When we say so, we are not philosophizing, we are stating the truth. The ultimate reality is before God all the time, and God speaks in the light of that reality.

The time factor in the Bible is one of the greatest problems to the human mind; yet it vanishes from one's horizon the moment there is an inward seeing of God's eternal thought concerning the Church.

Perhaps, in view of the above, you may ask: How do you account for the statement that the Church is sanctified or purified by the washing of water with the word (see Eph. 5.26)? Let us first observe the context. It tells us of how husband and wife should act. Love is required of the husband, and submission is required of the wife. The question is not how to be a husband, or how to be a wife, but, *being* a husband, how you should live; or, *being* a wife, how you should live. The point set forth is not that you must love in order to be a husband, or that you must obey to be a wife; but that being a husband you should love, or being a wife you should obey. Now the same principle applies in relation to the Church. The called-out ones are not washed in order *to be* the Church; they are washed because they *are* the Church. There is no question of sin here. The object of washing is not merely for cleansing, it is also for refreshment. The Church *has already been washed* (1 Cor. 6.11), so by washing she is kept fresh. The husband acts as a husband because he is a husband, the wife acts as a wife because she is a wife, the Church is washed because she has been washed. The Church has reached the standard, so she lives in correspondence with the standard. That which is not the Church could never become the Church by any amount of washing.

God sees the Church utterly pure, utterly perfect; and as we see that ultimate spiritual reality in heaven, we shall live in the power of that reality on earth.

6 | The Reality of the Church

Many Christians have seen the outward form of the Church, but they have never beheld the inward reality. They have no knowledge of the Church's essential nature. And hence the subject of the Church is regarded as a controversial one, which is to be studiously avoided for the sake of unity. Once I said to a Christian worker at Keswick in England: "Why does the Keswick Convention never mention the Church?" "Oh," he said, "because Keswick is for the deepening of the Christian life, of spiritual life." Hence, here, the Church and the spiritual life of the Christian are thought to be unrelated, whereas nothing is more intimately related to the spiritual life of the children of God than the Church. In fact, there is no such thing as spiritual life apart from the Church.

"Oh, to Be Like Thee" may be a hymn which the individual believer can sing, but not the Church, for the Church is the Body of Christ. There is no need for the Church to pray that she may be like Christ, for the

Church *is* Christ. When we see the true nature of the Church, our whole life will be revolutionized.

Most Christians admit that to struggle and strive after heavenliness is wrong, but still they struggle and strive because they think heavenliness is something to be attained. We may work our way across the Atlantic or the Pacific, but we cannot work our way from earth to heaven. Heaven is both the origin and the abode of the Church. The Church has never known any other sphere *than* heaven, so the question of striving to reach heaven can never arise in the Church. The Church has never known any other sphere than heaven. When Christ was on earth, He once declared: "No one hath ascended into heaven, but he that descended out of heaven, even the Son of man, who is in heaven" (John 3.13).

Heaven is not a place the Church will reach at some future date. The Church *is there* and was never anywhere else. Not till we see this fact do we know our heavenly calling. Our heavenly calling does not call us into heaven; rather, it makes known to us that we are already of heaven and in heaven.

The Church is not a company of Christians working their way heavenward, but a company of Christians who are actually now citizens of heaven. Alas! Christianity in the experience of most Christians is an endeavor to be what they are not, and an endeavor to do what they cannot do. They are always struggling to not love the world because at heart they really love it. They are always trying to be humble because at heart they are still proud. This is the experience of so-called Christianity, but it is not the experience of the Church.

The question of deliverance from the world or redemption from sin never arises in the Church, for the Church never had any connection with sin or with the world.

The Church existed before the foundation of the world and was never in the world, so she has never been touched by the Fall. Alas, the human mind cannot dissociate the thought of sin from the Church. But in the Divine mind, there is no relationship between sin and the Church. The Church infinitely transcends all thought of sin: in fact, the Church is the most positive thing in the universe. The Church is Christ. The Church has no connection with sin, and consequently no connection with redemption. Anything that calls for redemption does not belong to the Church. As individual believers, because we were born of Adam, we need redemption. It is not the Church that is redeemed, but we sinners who are redeemed; and being redeemed, we become part of the Church. In our experience the Church exists after redemption, but in the sight of God the church existed before redemption. Redemption relates to our standing in Adam; the Church relates to our standing in Christ. The Church is the One New Man where Christ is all and in all. The Church is Christ in corporate form.

The Church is not an organization, not something to be understood and attained to; it is something to be seen. When we see the heavenly reality of the Church, then we see our heavenly nature and we know that our starting-point as Christians is not earth but heaven.

The Church is perfect, perfect beyond any possibility of improvement. Theologians often say: "That perfection is the *standing* (or position) of the Church; but her *state* is not so." Yet in the sight of God there is no imperfection in the Church eternally. Why be bothered by the endless questions that relate to the old creation? They simply vanish when we see the reality of the Church. The Church is the sphere in which God exercises His authority on the earth; and today, even in the midst of a polluted universe, He has a sphere of unsullied purity for His abode.

PART THREE

FROM THE MINISTRY OF 1938–39*

*The two messages included in this Part were given by the author during a visit he made to England and Europe during 1938–39. —Editor

1 | The Limitations of God* (A Précis)

The eyes of Jehovah run to and fro throughout the whole earth, to show himself strong in the behalf of them whose heart is perfect toward him. (2 Chron. 16.9)

I came to cast fire upon the earth; and what do I desire, if it is already kindled? But I have a baptism to be baptized with; and how am I straitened till it be accomplished! (Luke 12.49–50)

... the church, which is his body, the fulness of him that filleth all in all. (Eph. 1.22c-23)

We think a great deal about the power, the omnipotence, of God, but we seldom think about the limita-

---

*This article, reprinted from the March-April 1953 issue of *A Witness and a Testimony* magazine published in London, England, is a message that was delivered in English by the author sometime during his visit to England and other European countries in 1938-39. Reprinted by permission of the Trustees of the Witness and Testimony Literature Trust, London.—*Editor*

tions of God. There are many things which the Lord cannot do today. Although He is omnipotent, He has limitations, and those limitations are clearly taught in His word. We will look at some examples:

"And he that was sown among the thorns, this is he that heareth the word; and the care of the world, and the deceitfulness of riches, choke the word, and he becometh unfruitful" (Matt. 13.22). We know the word of God is a mighty thing. It is God's declared will that it shall not return unto Him void; but we read that the word can be choked, it can be limited.

"O Jerusalem, Jerusalem, that killeth the prophets, and stoneth them that are sent unto her! how often would I have gathered thy children together, even as a hen gathered her chickens under her wings, and ye would not!" (Matt. 23.27) The Lord Jesus said, "I would . . . and ye would not." There was nothing wrong with the Lord himself, nor with His will, nor with His power to accomplish that will, but there was something on the side of man which had the power to limit the Lord himself.

"Because all those men that have seen my glory, and my signs, which I wrought in Egypt and in the wilderness, yet have tempted me these ten times, and have not hearkened to my voice; surely they shall not see the land which I sware unto their fathers, neither shall any of them that despised me see it: but my servant Caleb, because he had another spirit with him, and hath followed me fully, him will I bring into the land whereinto he went; and his seed shall possess it" (Num. 14.22–24). Jehovah himself declared time after time that the land was going to be given to His people, and He had the power to bring them in. But we see in this passage that the people had the power to defeat the purpose of God, to limit Him, so that He could not do what He had sworn to do.

"Behold, Jehovah's hand is not shortened, that it cannot save; neither his ear heavy, that it cannot hear: but your iniquities have separated between you and your God, and your sins have hid his face from you, so that he will not hear" (Is. 59.1-2). The hand of the Lord is not shortened, and the ear of the Lord is not deaf. Then why did He not save, why did He not hear? It was because of the sins and the iniquities of His people, which limited Him.

"Bring ye the whole tithe into the store-house, that there may be food in my house, and prove me now herewith, saith Jehovah of hosts, if I will not open you the windows of heaven, and pour you out a blessing, that there shall not be room enough to receive it" (Mal. 3.10). God wanted to bless the land of Israel with so much blessing that there would not be room to receive it, but He could not do it because the tithe had not been brought into His house.

"But he went out, and began to publish it much, and to spread abroad the matter, insomuch that Jesus could no more openly enter into the city, but was without in desert places: and they came to him from every quarter" (Mark 1.45 mg.). The Lord told this man, whom He had healed, not to say a word about it, but he began to blaze the matter abroad, with the result that the Lord could not enter the city, but had to shut himself away in desert places. Natural zeal limits the Lord.

"And he could there do no mighty work, save that he laid his hands upon a few sick folk, and healed them" (Mark 6.5). In this case, the Lord could do no mighty works because of unbelief.

In 2 Chronicles 16.9 we see that the Lord is looking for a man whose heart is perfect toward Him, to show himself strong on his behalf: so that we see that God is limited by an imperfect heart.

If you go through the word of God, you will find these facts established. God is omnipotent, but His omnipotence is subject to limitations. He must have conditions which are suitable to His working. The question is whether God is going to be limited, or is going to be unlimited. We have to learn through bitter experience that we cannot *help* God, but we have the full power to *hinder* Him. The Creator of heaven and earth can be bound by us, just flesh and blood! It is very serious. I trust the Lord will search our hearts and deal with us in a drastic way, so that we can see clearly if there is anything in us which is hindering and limiting His power. Are we willing to let go anything that may be a hindrance? Are we relying on sight and feeling, or are we living by faith in the living God? Are we trusting God—on the one hand to bring something out of nothing, and on the other hand to bring the dead back to life? Do we believe it, or does our lack of faith hinder Him from showing His power?

There are many things which may hinder, but it would not be profitable for us to attempt to deal with them here—we should get nowhere. The Lord must give us light, and light is certain if we abide in Him. It is not by self-examination—it is by coming to God alone:

and the difference between the two is the difference between heaven and earth. We will leave that just for now, and go on to something which is important.

Luke 12.49–50 is a passage speaking of the limitations of the Son of God while in the flesh on earth. The word "straitened" can be translated "crowded," "cramped," "not having a free way." The life, the power, of the Son of God was cramped in His body: He was limited by the condition of being in His body. For instance, He could not be at Jerusalem and Galilee at the same time. He was looking for the day when there would be a "baptism"—that is to say, His death on the cross—and when that came He would be released from the body of the flesh, and in resurrection would have a spiritual body that would not cramp Him, and His life could be imparted to His people.

That passage is exactly parallel to John 12.24–26, the grain of wheat falling into the ground and dying and bringing forth much fruit. There is life, there is power to reproduce, encaged [*sic*] in that grain—something which has been straitened, cramped, crowded: but when the grain dies, there is a great release, no more limitation. It will come up in much fruit.

The question of "the church, which is his body" comes in here. The body is for the full expression of the personality of the person. The Lord Jesus shows himself through each member of the Body, and He shows the whole of himself through the Church. When the Lord was in the flesh, He was moving in a fleshly body. Today He still manifests himself in a body, but now it is a spiritual Body, and we are the members. And as members of His Body, either we may be used to ex-press Him or we may limit Him. The Body is the way in which He expresses himself; He has no other way. This is a great responsibility. We are the only means of expression He has. That is why the utter Lordship of Christ is so very important. We have to come to the place where we are not in any way limiting Him: so that through His Body He may bring himself to bear on the world and on the spirit-world of evil powers. That is what the Lord is seeking in these days.

How does it come about that the omnipotence of God becomes limited by man? And will limitation be continued for eternity? We find in the word of God that in eternity past and eternity to come God is omnipotent and is not subject to limitation. But in the eternal purpose of God, He wants a people to share the life of His own Son and to manifest His Son. In order to bring this about, He created man, a free-willed being; and then the limitation of God began. There are now three wills at work, the Divine, the satanic and the human. God will not destroy the human will. He wants the will of the creature to be put on His side instead of on the side of Satan, and so He has accepted a position of limitation. If man is not on the side of God, God cannot do anything with him. God will not compel him to do anything.

But God is working toward a goal. There is One whose will is absolutely identified with the Father's. There is One who will not limit God; and by His death and resurrection His life is imparted to us. A Body is being formed by the power of the Spirit, and God is looking to the members of the Body to function in such a way that they will not limit Him — they will be respon-

sive to Him; and in this new creation, identified with
His will, His limitations will be for ever put out of the
way. God will be able to go back to His omnipotence
without limitation. We must first come to the place
where God has a free way in us, before He can bring
the whole creation back to that. The Church is a first
fruit in God's creation [see James 1.18], so what is going to be true universally in the kingdom-age should
be true at least of the overcoming company of the people of God today.

What is the kingdom? "Thy will be done in earth,
as it is in heaven" [see Matt. 6.10]. That means that there
will be no human will coming out to limit Him. When
the question of the will is settled, then the question of
power is also settled. What is the secret of really serv-
ing the Lord? It is not doing a hundred and one things
for the Lord. Service is really submission to the Lord —
knowing the true meaning of that word, "to obey is better than sacrifice" [1 Sam. 15.22b]. Abraham was one
who obeyed God's voice; and the Lord is after such utter responsiveness to himself, so that He can have a free
way unhindered.

May the Lord speak to our hearts and show us
whether there is anything there which will undermine
the sovereignty, the lordship and the headship of Jesus.
Once more let us say, Jesus is Lord!

2 | Divine Principles of Service*

Speak unto the children of Israel, and take of them rods, one for each fathers' house, of all their princes according to their fathers' houses, twelve rods: write thou every man's name upon his rod. And thou shalt write Aaron's name on the rod of Levi; for there shall be one rod for each head of their fathers' houses. And thou shalt lay them up in the tent of meeting before the testimony, where I meet with you. And it shall come to pass, that the rod of the man whom I shall choose shall bud: and

*This message, like the one presented in the previous chapter, was also delivered in English by the author, at a Workers' Conference during his lengthy visit to Britain and Europe in 1938–39. Unlike the previous message, which obviously had an editor's hand present (either that of the author himself or of someone else), the above message was printed "as spoken"—that is to say, there was no editing of the resultant text prior to publication. It originally appeared in the January–February 1939 issue of *A Witness and a Testimony* magazine, and is reprinted here by permission of the Trustees of the Witness and Testimony Literature Trust, London. Only a few insertions have now been added in brackets for clarity.—*Editor*

I will make to cease from me the murmurings of the
children of Israel, which they murmur against you. (Num.
17.2–5).

Jesus, when he was baptized, went up straightway from
the water: and lo, the heavens were opened unto him, and
he saw the Spirit of God descending as a dove, and coming upon him; and lo, a voice out of the heavens, saying,
This is my beloved Son, in whom I am well pleased. (Matt.
3.16–17).

Behold, I send forth the promise of my Father upon
you: but tarry ye in the city, until ye be clothed with power
from on high. (Luke 24.49).

The Basis of True Ministry

We come to consider the Divine principle of service of God. There are specific principles from which
no one who tries to serve the Lord can deviate. The principle which God laid down in His word for service to
Him is as definite as are the conditions of salvation.
We cannot change the conditions of salvation: no one
can ever get saved that way. Similarly, we cannot change
the conditions of service to God: no one will ever be
used by the Lord that way. The conditions for service
to God are just as specific as the conditions of salvation. The conditions of salvation, or, rather, the basis
of salvation, is upon the Lord's death and resurrection,
and on no other ground. The *ground* of His death and
resurrection is the ground of our acceptance with God.
The *principle* of the death and resurrection of the Lord
is the condition, is the basis of our service to God. Our

salvation rests on the *fact* of the death and the *fact* of the resurrection of our Lord, but our service is based on the *principle* of death; not the fact exactly, but the principle of death and the principle of the resurrection of our Lord.

By God's grace we want to see a little how the principle of the death and resurrection of the Lord Jesus governs our service to Him. No one could be a true servant without knowing the principle of the death and the principle of the resurrection. Even the Lord himself served on that ground. You will find in Matthew 3 that before the public ministry ever began our Lord was baptized. He was baptized, not because He had any sin or anything which needed cleansing, but still He was baptized. We know the meaning of baptism: it is death and resurrection. The ministry of the Lord did not begin until He was on that ground. It was after He had been baptized, had stood on the ground of being dead and resurrected, that He served, that He ministered.

We cannot do otherwise. The Spirit came down upon Him on the basis of His death and resurrection, and then He ministered. So we could safely say this, that all the work which our Lord did on earth prior to His actual death and resurrection was on the ground of death and resurrection, though actually Calvary and resurrection were still in the future. But everything He had been doing was on that ground. It was on the ground of baptism, that is, death and resurrection, that He worked. If the Son of Man has to go through death and resurrection in order to work, then no servant of the Lord today could serve the Lord without actually knowing the principle of death and resurrection. It is

out of the question altogether. The Lord made it very
clear for His servants when He went away. He had died,
and He has risen, and he told them to wait in Jerusalem
for the Spirit to come upon them.

Now what is this Spirit, this power from on high?
The power from on high for which those early disciples
were waiting was nothing less than the virtue of the
death and resurrection of the Lord. The power of the
Spirit is the virtue of the death and resurrection of the
Lord. To put it in another way, the Holy Spirit is the
vessel, so to speak, into which the death and resurrection of the Lord is put. He is the One who contains
that. That is the reason why the Spirit could not be given
before the Lord had been glorified. The Holy Spirit
could only be given when the Lord Jesus was glorified.
So it is only when this Spirit rests upon men and
women, that they can witness. Without the death and
resurrection as a basis there is no testimony possible,
and there will be no witnesses.

If we turn to the Old Testament we find the same
thing is there. I have referred to one passage which is
a very familiar one, the seventeenth of Numbers. The
question of Aaron's ministry is contested. There is a
great doubt among the people whether Aaron was truly
called of God. There is a doubt, a suspicion somewhere
about his ministry. The people say, Whether that man
is ordained of God or not we do not know! So God
sought to prove who is His servant and who is not; the
Lord set out to show who is His true minister. How?
Twelve dead rods were put before the Lord in the sanctuary over against the testimony, and they were there
for a night. Then the Lord said that the one which

budded and blossomed and brought forth fruit was the one chosen. We all know the meaning of that. The budding rod speaks of resurrection. Death and resurrection is the basis of true God-recognized ministry. Without that you have nothing. The budding of Aaron's rod proved him to be on a true basis. God will only recognize us as His ministers if we have truly gone through death and resurrection. No one can serve the Lord without being on resurrection ground.

I am going to try to come back to this a few minutes later, but at the present I want to get down to something more practical. It is very easy to receive something as a principle and admire it, and yet to lose out in that way. With all the admirations for the truth in our heart, we may yet not be blessed by it. So we will try to get down to some actual things, to see what it means to go through death and resurrection.

The Power of the Death of Christ

We know the death of the Lord works in different ways and in different aspects. We know how the death of the Lord has worked on the question of sins: I mean, as to our forgiveness. We all know that our forgiveness is based on His shed blood. If there is no blood shed there is no remission of sins. We see that death works as regards sins. Then I think Romans 6 will naturally come into view. We all know that our old man has been crucified. How? What is in view there? That we should not serve sin. Here you find it is not sins which are in view but sin, the power of sin. Many of us, I trust, have

seen that. At some time in your life the Lord opened
your eyes to see that your old man has been crucified,
and you almost shouted for joy and praised the Lord
that that terrible old man which you tried to deal with
for years, and over which you had failed, has been dealt
with on the cross, and henceforth sin will never dom-
inate. That is the death of the Lord as to the question
of sin in its power, in its operation in us, and that is
most precious. We do not want to under-estimate that,
but still, even that does not touch the core of the question we are going to talk about. Bless God, we have
to begin by death, and death to sin is our initial step
into the service of God, but that does not make us real
God-recognized servants. We bless God for Romans 6,
but then people see Romans 6 only with sin in view.
The power of sin has been destroyed because the old
man has been dealt with, but that does not touch the
question yet.

Further on you will find that when once that question has been settled and you could freely reckon what
has happened in the Lord, then the question of yielding
comes in. The question of self-will, of human will arises,
the question of consecration, so to speak, or surrender,
and death works that way. Death works in a way that
I am willing to let go my will, I am willing to obey the
Lord. Praise God, Romans 6 is a real blessing, and we
praise God also with all our hearts for our yielding that
day when we came to God and said, Yes! and bade
goodbye for ever to our sins. We praise God for that
day; we remember how we came to Him and dealt with
the question of our wills. The will has been touched,
and death works there. That constitutes a ground for

our ministry, but still that does not touch the core of the question.

Thus the third realm where the death of the Lord touched is still not enough. I do not mean to say it is not precious; because it was a red letter day when we got over to God's side and refused to live on ourselves. But you find many really consecrated saints who do not know what is their natural life. There will be consecration, there may be surrender, but there is still the lack of the knowledge of what is meant by soul.

Then there is another aspect which is quite popular and known to many, the aspect which is presented in Romans 7. I would like to call it the fourth one. There you find it is not a question of sins that is in view, nor the question of sin, nor that of the will, but there the question of holiness of life is in view.

In chapter 7 you find a true man of God trying to please God in righteousness. The whole question in Romans 7 is not service, but it is living holiness, personal holiness. I want to serve God with my life; I want to be a holy man, so to speak; I want to live a righteous life! But that brother got it all wrong. What did he do? He came under the power of the law. That means he tried to serve the Lord with his own power, with his natural power. Now mark you, there is a great difference between natural power as spoken of in Romans 7 and natural power as we are going to speak of it. Of course, I believe there is a link, but still there is a distinction between the word. There in Romans 7 you find a man not exactly having the question of ministry before him at all. The whole question is of obeying the law. The law may demand something that I shall not desire, I must not desire. This man tried to live up to that by his own power, and that power was exercised to please God in his daily living, and he failed. The cross has to be known in that aspect also. It has to come in to deal with us, so that we say, "I cannot please God, so I will not please God." Do not misunderstand me. The cross has to bring you to a point where you will say, "I cannot do anything, therefore I will not do anything; I cannot please God, therefore from henceforth I am not going to please God." But that does not mean that you will not please God at all. The thing is *I* will not do it. *I* know it is utter futility to do it, to serve the Lord with *my* powers, trying to come up to His standard of life. So the cross cuts here also into my natural power as trying to please God in my life. I refuse to have anything to do with that, I will only trust the Spirit to bring that out in me. I am not going to produce that for God, I will trust God to produce that in me.

I believe some of us have passed through deep waters to find this. One has gone through much trying, and trying, and ever trying to get somewhere and yet getting nowhere, and thus has come to a realization of the futility of it all, and to the point where we say, " Lord, I cannot do it, I can only trust Thee to bring that out." Then you have the death of the Lord working that way.

But with all these being known, and actually known in experience, we are still left somewhere concerning our experience of the principle of His death. There is still one realm, one sphere, which the death of the Lord must actually enter before we are really of use to Him. Even with all these experiences we are still unsafe for Him to use us. How many servants of the Lord are used by the Lord to build twelve feet and then they try to pull down fifteen feet, as we Chinese put it. You are used in a sense, but at the same time you destroy your own work because of there being somewhere something undealt with. So we [will] try to get at the point at this time. May the Lord give us grace to see what it is which must be dealt with.

The Question of Soul Energy

It is a question of soul, in terms of natural energy. Please remember, the question of soulish energy is quite different from what we have already mentioned. Even those points which we have already touched upon do not make us know actually what is the death to the soul energy; there is still something else. So please do not mix these things up. We do not want to go into a lot of analysis, but still you have to keep the distinction. Soul energy as to the service to God is quite different from those which we have mentioned.

Now what is this soul? Everything that is natural! I do not know how you have been, and how you pass through, but personally, I could speak for myself. I find it to be one of the costliest things to go into, and I have to confess that it is one of the most difficult things to realize, because one is so very easily deceived even by oneself in this respect. Also, when one has got just a little initial experience one could easily pretend to have the whole experience, to think one knows more than one really does. So I would like by God's grace that we should tread slowly and try to find out how we should deal with it.

What is this soul power or natural energy? It is simply this, what *you* can do, what *you* are yourself, what *you* have from nature. The power of soul is present with us all. Those who have been taught by the Lord repudiate that principle as a life principle: they refuse to live by it; they will not let it reign; they will not allow it to be the power-spring of the work of God. But those who have not been taught of God rely upon it: they utilize it; they think it is *the* power.

Let us illustrate. I take my mind. I had a keen mind: there you have the soul power, the natural energy. What is the natural energy? Natural energy is something you have apart from new birth. Before new birth you had it naturally. Something comes with your natural birth, something is developed from your natural birth, something coming out from the natural birth is being used as a kind of capability to produce things. That is natural life, that is the natural energy. Now the trouble is here. We get converted, we have new birth, a deep work of God has been effected in our spirits. God is the Father of our spirits. Something has been done, an essential union has been effected in our spirits. But there you are! on the one hand I have an essential union with God in my spirit, and yet at the same time I carry something with me which I get from my natural birth. Now what am I going to do with it?

The general tendency is this: formerly I used to use my mind to pore over history, over business, over chemistry, over questions of the world, over literature, over poetry; I tried to study with it, using my keen mind to get something out of it; now my desire has been changed, so I employ the same mind in the things of

God. I have changed my subject of interest, but I have not changed my heart. The whole thing is this: the subject of interest has been utterly changed (Praise God for that!), but that is not enough. We utilize the same power which we used before to pursue history and geography to study Corinthians and Ephesians. The same power is used, but that is not of God. God will not allow that. The trouble with so many saints is that they have only changed their subject of interest, they have not changed their power and energy. This is only by way of illustration.

You will find that there are many things we carry into Divine service. Take the question of eloquence. There are some who are really born orators, they can present their case very well. Then they get converted, and they think they will employ the same power for preaching. It is a different subject, but the same power.

We cannot see this simply by hearing. God must come in and put His finger on something which He sees, and say, Look here, this is natural, this is something belonging to the old creation, this must go. Unless He puts His finger on something in us and points that out to us as being natural we cannot deal with it, we cannot see it. We may agree, assent, but we cannot see it. God has to come in to do something in the most deliberate and thorough way, in a way which will rule out everything.

Coming to a point, we have to say, "Lord, it is unclean, it is impure." That word purity is a blessed word. I always associate it with the Spirit. Purity means something altogether out from the Spirit. Impurity means mixture. Then the question comes, What is this natural life? How am I to deal with it? The fundamental thing is I must have revelation. I must see it. I can tell you this, that one could understand it for years without actually seeing it. You can rejoice in the truth, but you will never loathe yourself; rejoice in the teaching, but never loathe yourself. When God comes in, when He gives a revelation, when you see that the natural life is something God cannot use in His service, and He shows the corruptness and impurity of the whole thing, then you will find you will not enjoy the truth; you will loathe yourself for what is in you, for what is going on with you. Then there will be deliverance later, but not until you have that. That natural energy has to be dealt with.

God Alone to Have Glory

I have often asked something which I feel is very difficult. What is the reason that God wanted to do everything? For the whole point is that God wanted to do everything. He has done everything as regards our salvation, and He will do everything as regards our service. He will not let us have any part in it, either in the question of salvation or in the question of our service so far as ability is concerned. Why? If God is going to have all the glory, God has to do all the work; if He can share with you His work, He can share with you His glory. If he is going to have all the glory, He is going to do all the work. So He has to rule out everything that is of man, so that He may have the glory.

Of course, there is something more. Anything that

is out of us will never be truly fruitful, and will have no real spiritual value. As regards the eternal purpose, the full end of God, unless God is doing it no one can do it, we are out of it altogether. Natural energy fails us here; at its best it will fail.

A Dark Night

So here we come to the question of the rod, which was brought into the sanctuary for a night, a dark night, without seeing anything, and then in the morning it budded. There you have the death and the resurrection. This aspect of the death of the Lord, spoken of in the Scriptures as our conformity to His death, is just like the death which our Lord died in the sense of John 12, the grain of wheat. He passed away, and His life emerges into many lives. The Son died, and came out to be "many sons." One grain died, and you will have many grains. Many grains were actually in that grain, but that grain is now becoming, not many grains, but the first grain. Once upon a time it is the grain of wheat; now the grain becomes the first grain. So we find the only begotten Son of God becomes ["the firstborn, among many brethren" — Rom. 8.29], and we are coming in as His brethren, we have a share in His life. It is in this aspect of death we died. We lose our life, so that we may pass on life to others. We may be life-imparting ones, giving our life to others.

Now the question of death and the natural energy is this: The natural life, the natural energy will continue with us until our death, but there must be a fundamental breaking of that life, of that power, of that energy just as God touched the sinew of Jacob. He continued to walk, but he continued to be lame. He has his feet on him, but the life has been touched, and from that wound Jacob has never recovered. God has to bring us to a point—I do not know how, but God will—to deal with us so that our natural power is cut off. Some of us He has to deal with very harshly, in difficult ways, to bring us through to a point where we dare not trust ourselves, where we are almost afraid to trust ourselves. We come to a point where we do not like to do things.

I can tell you this, that for a year after I was converted I had a lust to preach; it was impossible to stay silent. It seemed as if there was something going on and one had to go on. Then one day that has been touched, and you do not do it because you want to do it, but because the Lord wants it. When that natural life has not been dealt with, you have a lust to preach, and yet sometimes the Lord cannot move you to do one thing. You are living by the natural life, and that natural life varies a good deal. When emotionally you are set on this way you go at full speed; when emotionally you are set on going the other way you will not move at all even when duty calls. You are not pliable in the Lord's hands. He has to take the natural energy out of you so that you will do it because He wants it, not because you like it. You may like it, or you may dislike it, but you will do it just the same. It is not that I can derive a certain joy out of preaching, out of this work, out of that work, therefore I do it; it is because this is the will of God, therefore I do it—with joy, or without joy. You will be coming to a place where God can have His way with you because the natural side of your energy has been dealt with. God is out for this. It may be a painful process with some of us, or it may be just one stroke. But God has His ways, and we must have regard for them. Every true servant of God must know that touch of that wound from which he can never recover. There must be that in effect in you, that from henceforth you will be afraid of yourself, you will be afraid to do anything. You know what kind of sovereign dealing you will get if you do it, you know what a bad time you will have before the Lord if you do move out from yourself. You will immediately find God's hand is upon you, He will never let you free.

And then you come to a place which we speak of as resurrection ground. Death in principle has to be wrought out in a crisis to our natural lives, and then you will find God releases you into resurrection, you will come out on resurrection ground. What does it mean? You will find that what you have lost is coming back, though not as before; it is your life-principle that is at work, something that empowers and strengthens you, something which is animating you, giving you life. From henceforth what you have lost will be coming back under [resurrection] power. For instance, if we want to be spiritual there is no need for us to amputate our hands or feet; we can have our body. So we can have our soul, the full use of our faculties, but it is not our life-spring; we are not living in it, we are not living by it, we use it. When the body becomes the life of man, we live like beasts. When the soul becomes the life of man we live as rebels from God, we live apart from the life of God. When we have to live our life in the spirit, and by the spirit, we use our soul faculties just as we use our physical faculties.

But the difficulty with many is that night. The Lord graciously laid me aside once in my life, quite a long number of months, and put me into utter darkness, almost as if He had forsaken me and nothing was going on, as if it was the end of everything; and then He brought back things bit by bit. The temptation is always to take things back ourselves, but the point is there must be a full night in the sanctuary, a full night in darkness. It cannot be hurried. He knows how long that must be. We would like to have death and resurrection put together within one hour of each other, we cannot stand the thought that God will keep us aside for that while. We cannot stay that long. I do not know how long it will be, but in principle I think it is quite safe to say this, that there will be a period when God will simply put you there. It will seem as if nothing is happening, everything is going. It will seem as if you are coming against a blank wall and you are losing out; you think every other one has been blessed and used and you yourself are left high and dry. Lie quiet: it is all in darkness, but it is only a night really. It may be a night, but it is only a night. After that you will find you will come up in glorious resurrection. The Lord is now at this time trying to touch us on this very question concerning our natural energy.

Discernment between Soul and Spirit of Paramount Importance

I think many of us have really found that there is a terrible need of real spiritual discernment amongst the children of God. I would like to ask the question, What is the root cause of lack of discernment? Why can we not differentiate and say, This is of God! and, This is not of God! Man is doing it all! or, This is God who is doing it! Why are there so many mistakes being made, so much that is of man being put down to be of God? What is the reason? It is simply because there is the lack of the distinction between spirit and soul in our lives, so that we cannot see it. It is only when our natural powers have been dealt with [that] we know what it means, and how costly it is; then every movement, every prompting of the natural man in others will be noticed without any effort. You have passed through. I do not mean to say that we will learn the lesson in order to notice the weaknesses of others, but in Divine service there is that necessity for differentiating between the natural and the spiritual. We do not want just to have an experience of our own, so that we can sit on the platform and criticize others in a more competent way, but we do want to know something that is utterly of God, that has nothing to do with man's trying to deal with the matter in its fundamental cause; and then spontaneously you can see what is of man and what is of God.

I have always thought that there is only one way to true spiritual discernment; that is, dealing with the natural life in yourself. The lack of discernment betrays the lack of a deep work in us. If we cannot see it in our own lives we can never see it in others. The beam has to be removed in order that the mote can be discovered. The Lord made that clear [see Matt. 7.1–5]. When the beam has been removed the mote will be discovered. May the Lord grant us grace, make us willing and ready to see there is a big realm in our own lives which needs a drastic dealing by God. Do not take anything for granted because you know something of Romans 6 in the question of sin or sins, or even the question of surrender. There is [still] that natural power which we are exerting every day and putting into Divine service.

Some who have a bigger soul than others will have a more difficult time. I think some of you may know that verse in 1 Thessalonians which is a very important one. There is a word there which says, "Encourage the fainthearted" [5.14]; and some versions put it, "Encourage the feebleminded." But in fact that word "feebleminded" or "fainthearted" in the Greek means "the small-souled." Encourage the small-souled. So I think it is Scriptural to infer from this that there are those who are only small-souled, and there are those who are naturally big-souled, and the big-souled people will have a more difficult time. We cannot blame them, but we have to say that this is true. The Lord will deal with you in a most drastic way to get that life out of you.

I remember once someone said this to me. He tried to introduce me to someone, and said, "I understand the Lord has used our brother to save quite a number of souls." Then I turned to the one who introduced me and said, "Brother, that is the worst introduction I have ever got." He said, "What do you mean?" I said, "Do you mean to say the Lord used me to save souls? You mean the Lord used me to win souls." Winning souls and saving souls are very different things. We win souls as men being won to Christ, but we do not save souls.

Souls must be lost. Throughout the New Testament, is there anything telling you that you must save your soul? It is always said that you must lose your soul [e.g., Matt. 10.38–39, where the word translated life is actually soul in the original Greek — hence soul life]. Blessed be His Name! We are willing to lose it, to part with it, to let it go. May the Lord give us grace to face this question of soul, and come to a place where we can say, I have lost it!* And yet it is a lifelong process, it will continue. Maybe today the Lord will put His finger upon someone and say, There is another department which you have never entered before. But the point is, that fundamental touch, that fundamental wound, that life-wound, must be received.

May the Lord give us grace.

---

*Of course, the author here is not declaring the annihilation of the soul or the non-use of its faculties, but the disabling of the natural life or energy that animates the soul so that it may be animated instead by the resurrection life of Christ. This is made clear by the author in the subsection above entitled "A Dark Night." —*Editor*

TITLES YOU
WILL WANT TO HAVE

by Watchman Nee

Basic Lesson Series
Volume 1 — A Living Sacrifice
Volume 2 — The Good Confession
Volume 3 — Assembling Together
Volume 4 — Not I, But Christ
Volume 5 — Do All to the Glory of God
Volume 6 — Love One Another

The Church and the Work
Volume 1 — Assembly Life
Volume 2 — Rethinking the Work
Volume 3 — Church Affairs

Worship God
Interpreting Matthew
Back to the Cross
The Character of God's Workman
Gleanings in the Fields of Boaz
The Spirit of the Gospel
The Life That Wins
From Glory to Glory
The Spirit of Judgment
From Faith to Faith
The Lord My Portion
Aids to "Revelation"
Grace for Grace
The Better Covenant
A Balanced Christian Life
The Mystery of Creation
The Messenger of the Cross
Full of Grace and Truth — Volume 1
Full of Grace and Truth — Volume 2
The Spirit of Wisdom and Revelation
Whom Shall I Send?
The Testimony of God
The Salvation of the Soul
The King and the Kingdom of Heaven
The Body of Christ: A Reality
Let Us Pray
God's Plan and the Overcomers
The Glory of His Life
"Come, Lord Jesus"
Practical Issues of This Life
Gospel Dialogue
God's Work
Ye Search the Scriptures
The Prayer Ministry of the Church
Christ the Sum of All Spiritual Things
Spiritual Knowledge
The Latent Power of the Soul
Spiritual Authority
The Ministry of God's Word
Spiritual Reality or Obsession
The Spiritual Man

by Stephen Kaung

Discipled to Christ
The Splendor of His Ways
Seeing the Lord's End in Job
The Songs of Degrees
Meditations on Fifteen Psalms

ORDER FROM:

Christian Fellowship Publishers, Inc.
11515 Allecingie Parkway
Richmond, Virginia 23235